HOBBYMAN

Easy Conversational English With An Alien

Written by Simon Thollar
Illustrations by YUJI

丸善プラネット

ACKNOWLEDGEMENT

Thanks to Kyoko and Zac for help and time.
Also, thanks to Superman for inspiration.
Special thanks to Nao (a.k.a. Yoko) for help with
the video and Yuji for his magnificent illustrations.

DEDICATION

I dedicate this book to Keiji Kobayashi,
a great and inspired teacher.

This textbook was wholly produced on a *Macintosh*.
The word processing package used was *Nisus Writer*.

Why Hobbyman?

This is an English textbook. The main character is called Hobbyman. Hobbyman is from another planet, and came to Earth to learn about hobbies. This text has been written, around that theme.

It is aimed at people who have studied English before, but never really understood, and still haven't come to grips with, the basics. While this particular textbook is directed at Japanese students of English, it can be argued that progressing on to more advanced English without really understanding the basics yields little or no reward. It is this author's contention that this is so. This book aims to develop English concepts already learned, or at least, taught, in the earlier compulsory Japanese high school English syllabus.

There are a total of 15 lessons, in Hobbyman. Each lesson is based on a hobby or sport. Using this idea as a theme to tie the book together, a number of important basic language points are introduced into each lesson. With the final lesson serving as a revision chapter, the fundamental points taught in the first 14 lessons can be reviewed by the student to check his or her total understanding.

While there is invariably some new material taught, the emphasis is strongly based on utilizing words and structures which should be already familiar to the student. The intention is to reinforce what is already more or less known, not to add new material, and thus build on a possibly shaky foundation. Anyone who may disagree with this particular pedagogical philosophy need only talk to any foreign student of English to see that the student's theoretical knowledge will far outweigh both his or her practical knowledge and their ability to use what they think they know. Such students know what they want to say, but don't know how to say it.

Lewis Carol reputedly once said *When I use a word, I choose it to mean exactly what I want it to; nothing more and nothing less.* Sadly, words mean nothing if they can't be logically construed to make a comprehensible sentence. To that end, this text attempts to redress the imbalance caused by those people who insist on teaching more and more advanced material without ever really making sure that elementary concepts, words and forms are understood.

The creation of the character *Hobbyman* was based on the author's belief that peoples' pastimes or hobbies are always a source of interest to other people who know little or nothing about them. Also, learning, if enjoyable, is not a chore. The character *Hobbyman* seemed like a good way to tie a number of hobbies into a coherent theme suitable for a textbook, in an enjoyable way. I hope you agree.

S.T.   Feb 1995

CONTENTS:

To the student:
This book is written for you. It is called **Hobbyman**. I hope you find it interesting.

Why this book?
Most of the material in this text is **not** new. You have probably learnt it at some time - maybe junior high school, maybe senior high school - maybe even last year. I believe that many people cannot improve their English because they have problems with **basics**. I am **not** talking about grammar. I am talking about words or phrases which you have learnt but don't really understand. This book **reviews** those basic words and phrases. If you are able to understand them, you will greatly improve your everyday conversational English skills.

How to use it:
The best way to use this book is **read it**! Even if you think you understand some lessons, **read them again**. Do the student exercises.

Help?
Chapter 15 is a cross-referenced review chapter. When you finish the book, read chapter 15. Every language note from lessons 1 to 14 appears in chapter 15, with the page numbers where they were first introduced. Read them. Can you remember the meaning of each one? There are 172!! If you can't remember one, read about it again. If you can remember and understand them all, congratulations!

Anything else?
English **is** fun. Don't worry if you don't understand everything perfectly. Just do your best. You might even learn something . . .

S.T.

Hi, my name is Hobbyman. I'm from the planet Nohobby. On the planet Nohobby, there are no hobbies. Everybody works very hard. Nobody has any time for hobbies. Life is very boring. I left my planet to travel around the universe and learn what people like doing in their free time. I have been to many planets and studied many peoples' hobbies. Soon, I have to go back to Nohobby and tell everybody about all the interesting hobbies I have seen.

I come to Earth because I wanted to learn about your hobbies. I have to go home soon, so this was the last planet I could visit. I was very lucky here, and I met many interesting people and saw many interesting hobbies. Please let me tell you about them.

First, I met Eric the guitarist. He told me about guitars. Then I met Shaun the surfer. He told me all about surfing. After that, I met Brick the card player and a guy that makes his own beer. Then I met a swimmer called Mark, a snowboarder called Burton and a martial arts expert called Bruce. They were all really nice guys.

Then I met a really weird tennis player called Boris, a talking computer called Mac and a guy that couldn't rollerblade very well. After that, I met a guy that was crazy about fishing, a man called John that really loved his car and Dale the mountain bike rider.

Finally, I met a pretty girl and her lazy boyfriend. He stayed on the sofa all day!

It was really interesting and I learnt a lot about hobbies and how to use free time. When I go back to Nohobby, I'll tell everybody about the nice people I met and the interesting hobbies I saw. Soon, we'll have hobbies even on Nohobby.

Anyway, thanks Earthpeople. Maybe I'll see you again. G'bye.

DID YOU KNOW THAT ...

Did you know that the guitar is over 400 years old. At first, the guitar had only 5 strings and was played in France and Italy. About 200 years ago, the 6 string guitar became popular in Germany. Now the guitar is popular all over the world. Some people say that the electric guitar is the most popular musical instrument in the world. There are over 1 million guitars in Japan!

1: GUITAR

LESSON FOCUS: the question word "HOW "

♪❷🎥

1 - 1. Dialogue: Hobbyman meets a guitarist.

1   **Hobbyman:**   Hi!
2   **Guitarist:**   Hi! How' you doing?[1]
3   **Hobbyman:**   Good thanks.[2] How about you?[3]
4   **Guitarist:**   Okay. How come you're wearing that cape?[4]
5   **Hobbyman:**   Ah . . . I'm Hobbyman. I'm not from Earth. I'm from the planet *Nohobby*.
6   **Guitarist:**   Yeah? I'm Eric. How do you do?[5] How did you come here?[6]
7   **Hobbyman:**   I flew.
8   **Guitarist:**   Yeah? How come you came to Earth?
9   **Hobbyman:**   Well . . . On my planet, there are no hobbies. I came here because I want to learn about hobbies. Anyway, what are you doing?
10 **Guitarist:**   I'm playing the guitar.
11 **Hobbyman:**   Guitar? How do you play the guitar?
12 **Guitarist:**   You put your fingers on the strings and pluck.
13 **Hobbyman:**   How many strings are there?[7]
14 **Guitarist:**   Just six. An electric bass has four and some acoustics have twelve.
15 **Hobbyman:**   Wow! How old were you when you started playing?[8]
16 **Guitarist:**   Well, I'm 28 now. I started playing 8 years ago. So, how do you like the guitar?[9]
17 **Hobbyman:**   It sounds really good. Anyway Eric, I gotta' go now.
18 **Guitarist:**   Okay Hobbyman, but before you go, how about a coffee?[10]
19 **Hobbyman:**   Thanks, but I really gotta' go. Maybe next time. Thanks again and goodbye.
20 **Guitarist:**   Yeah, see ya' around,[11] Hobbyman.

1 - 2. Short Dialogues: More "**how**" sentences.

A: <u>How's everything</u>?
B: <u>Not bad</u>, thanks. <u>How 'bout you</u>?
A: I'm <u>good thanks</u>.

*   *   *

A: John, this is Paul. Paul, John.
B: <u>How do you do</u>, John.
A: <u>It's nice to meet you</u> too, Paul.

*   *   *

A: <u>How</u> do you whistle, Humphrey?
B: Just put your lips together and
blow, Lauren.

*   *   *

A: <u>How</u> do you spell "Cherokee"?
B: C-H-E-R-O-K-E-E, I think.

*   *   *

A: <u>How many</u> shoes do you have,
Mrs. Marcos?
B: I have over 3000 pairs.

*   *   *

A: <u>How old</u> are you now, Ms. Gold?
B: I'm one hundred and two.

*   *   *

A: <u>How often</u> do you go skiing?
B: I usually go skiing every
Saturday and Sunday.

*   *   *

A: <u>How much</u> was your guitar?
B: It cost three hundred and
ninety eight dollars, Jimmy.

*   *   *

A: John is going to America.
B: <u>How come</u>?
A: He wants to meet Elvis.

*   *   *

A: <u>How come</u> you're not
getting married, Rie?
B: Because I don't love him.

*   *   *

A: <u>How</u> did you come here?
B: I came by car, today.

*   *   *

A: <u>How do you like</u> tennis,
Boris?
B: I love tennis, Peter.

*   *   *

A: <u>How about</u> a dance, baby?
B: No way! Leave me alone!

*   *   *

A: <u>How about</u> coming for a ride
with me, on my scooter?
B: No thanks, Takeshi.

*   *   *

1 - 3. New Vocabulary: Do you know these words?

Acoustic: An **acoustic** guitar is a hollow, non-electric guitar.
Cape: A **cape** is the same as a *mantle*. Superman & Batman use **capes**.
Planet: We live on the **planet** Earth.
Pluck: **Pluck** means to pull the strings on a guitar to make a noise.

1 - 4. Language Notes: Language Notes

How' you doing?[1]

How is an important word in greetings. There are many ways of saying **How are you.** For example, as you can see in long dialogue 1 - 1, we can say **How (are) you doing.** The following are all the same.

> **How** are you?
> **How** are you doing? ⟶ **How'** you doing?
> **How** are you going? ⟶ **How'** you going?
> **How**'s everything?

How' you doing is more common in American English, while **How' you going** is more common in British and Australian English.

Good thanks.[2]

If somebody says **How' you doing,** you can say **I'm good thanks.** You can also say **I'm good, good thanks** or just **good!** Try some other adjectives.

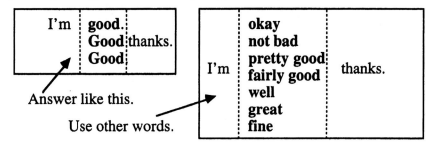

I'm	good.	
	Good	thanks.
	Good	

Answer like this.

Use other words.

I'm	okay	
	not bad	
	pretty good	
	fairly good	thanks.
	well	
	great	
	fine	

How about you?[3]

How about you means *And you?* **How about whisky** means *And whisky?* Look at the diagram to understand these uses.

A:	How you doing?	**A:**	Do you like beer?
B:	Okay. **How about you?**	**B:**	Sure.
A:	I'm good thanks.	**A:**	**How about whisky?**
		B:	Yeah, I like whisky too.

How come you're wearing that cape?[4]

How come is the same as *Why*. **How come you're wearing that cape** is the same as *Why are you wearing that cape*. Look at the following examples.

How come you're leaving?	→ Why are you leaving?
How come you came here?	→ Why did you come here?
How come he's not coming?	→ Why isn't he coming?
How come?	→ Why?

How do you do?[5]

When we meet somebody for the first time, we often shake hands and say **How do you do**. This is very polite. You can also say **(It's) nice to meet you**. This is more casual. Look at the diagram for other examples.

Very Polite	More Casual
How do you do?	(It's) **nice** to meet you. (It's) **good** to meet you. (It's) **great** to meet you. (I'm) **glad** to meet you. (I'm) **pleased** to meet you. (I'm) **happy** to meet you.

How did you come here?[6]

This is the basic **How** sentence. We can use it with any **verb**. This **How** means **By what method** or **In what way**. Look at the following diagram.

How did she come here?	→ She came by bus.
How do you play the horn?	→ Blow into the mouth piece.
How did you learn French?	→ I lived in France for 2 years.

How many strings are there?[7]

How many and **How much** both refer to number. **How many** refers to things that we can count. **How much** refers to things that we can't count. Look at the following diagram.

How many strings are there?	→ There are six.
How many brothers do you have?	→ I have three.
How much money do you have?	→ I have no money.
How much rain fell yesterday?	→ About 30 cms.

How old were you when you started playing?[8]

Other phrases, such as **How old** or **How long** refer to age or time or length. Look at the diagram.

How old is she now?	→ She's ten, I think.
How old was he when he met her?	→ He was twenty.
How long are your skis?	→ Mine are one ninety's.
How long has he known her?	→ About 20 years.

How do you like the guitar?[9]

We can ask peoples' opinions by saying **How do you like . . . ?** Look at the following diagram.

How do you like tennis?	I love tennis.
How do you like Sapporo beer? →	I think it's great.
How did you like travelling in Peru?	I had a really good time.

How about a coffee?[10]

We can also use **How about** as an invitation. For example, **How about a coffee** means *Would you like a coffee?*. **How about something to eat** means *Would you like something to eat?*. Look at the diagram.

A:	How about a coffee?	**A:**	How about something to eat?
B:	Yes please. Black, no sugar.	**B:**	No thanks. I'm not hungry.

See ya' around.[11]

Don't just say **Good-Bye** to your friends. You can say things like **See ya' 'round** (See you around), **See ya' 'bout** (See you about), **See ya' later** (See you later), **Catch ya' later** (Catch you later) or **Check ya' later** (Check you later).

♫☻🎥

1 - 5. Student Exercises: Fill in the blanks.
Choose the best sentence from the list on the next page.

1 **Reporter:** Hey, Superman. [   ]
2 **Superman:** About 20 years, I think.
3 **Reporter:** Okay. [   ]
4 **Superman:** My planet was destroyed.
5 **Reporter:** I see. [   ]
6 **Superman:** This "S" T-shirt is part of my image. [   ]

7	**Reporter:**	It's very nice, Superman. [＿＿＿＿＿＿＿]
8	**Superman:**	I have more than 20.
9	**Reporter:**	[＿＿＿＿＿＿＿]
10	**Superman:**	I flew.
11	**Reporter:**	[＿＿＿＿＿＿＿]
12	**Superman:**	Only 3 hours. I'm a quick flyer!
13	**Reporter:**	Wow. Okay, one last question. [＿＿＿＿]
14	**Superman:**	I turned 87 last week.

Choose the best sentences for the blanks.
a)　　　How come you came to Earth?
b)　　　How long did it take?
c)　　　How long have you been living on Earth?
d)　　　How old are you?
e)　　　How did you come to Earth?
f)　　　How many T-shirts do you have?
g)　　　How come you wear that "S" T-shirt?
h)　　　How do you like it?

1 - 6.　Student Exercise: Select the best answer.

1.　　The answer is **I'm good thanks**. What's the question?
　　　(a)　How doing?　　　　　(b)　How's it doing?
　　　(c)　How's you doing?　　(d)　How 'you doing?

2.　　Another way of saying **Why did you come** is:
　　　(a)　How come you come?　(b)　How come you came?
　　　(c)　How came you came?　(d)　How came you come?

3.　　When you meet someone for the first time, you can say:
　　　(a)　How are you do?　　　(b)　How do you?
　　　(c)　How do you do?　　　(d)　How come you do?

4.　　When you meet someone for the first time, you can say **Nice to meet you**. Which of the following is NOT the same?
　　　(a)　Good to meet you.　　(b)　Pleased to meet you.
　　　(c)　Glad to meet you.　　(d)　Fun to meet you.

5.　　It was snowing all day, yesterday. Which question is best?
　　　(a)　How many snows fell?　(b)　How much snows fell?
　　　(c)　How many snow fell?　(d)　How much snow fell?

6. If you want to ask somebody their opinion about golf, you can say:
    (a)   How like golf?   (b)   How do you think about golf?
    (c)   How do you think golf? (d)   How do you like golf?

7. If you want to offer somebody a coffee, you can say:
    (a)   How about a coffee?   (b)   How much is coffee?
    (c)   How are you coffee?   (d)   How come a coffee?

8. If you want to know how to make sushi, you can ask:
    (a)   How to make sushi?   (b)   How do you sushi?
    (c)   How do you make sushi? (d)   How can I sushi?

9. A friend says he likes tennis. You want to ask him if he likes squash too. What do you ask?
    (a)   How come squash?   (b)   How like squash?
    (c)   How is squash?   (d)   How about squash?

10. Instead of saying **Good-bye**, you can say **See you**. Which of the following is NOT the same?
    (a)   Watch you later.   (b)   See you later.
    (c)   Catch you later.   (d)   See ya' 'round.

1 - 7. Review of this lesson's major points. Do you understand these questions and expressions?

How' you doing?	How about you?
How come you're wearing that cape?	How do you do?
How did you come here?	How many strings are there?
How old is your guitar?	How do you like my car?
How about a coffee?	How do you spell "guitar"?
How come?	How often do you go dancing?

1 - 8. Student Exercise: STEREOGRAM. Can you see the hidden answer?

Hobbyman:	How often do you play guitar?
Guitarist:	Everyday, for one or two hours.
Hobbyman:	And how many guitars do you have?
Guitarist:	I've got 4 guitars; 2 electrics and 2 acoustics.
Hobbyman:	And how much did that guitar cost?
Guitarist:	Ahh . . . that guitar cost (. . . . .).

To find the price of the guitar, please look at the stereogram carefully.

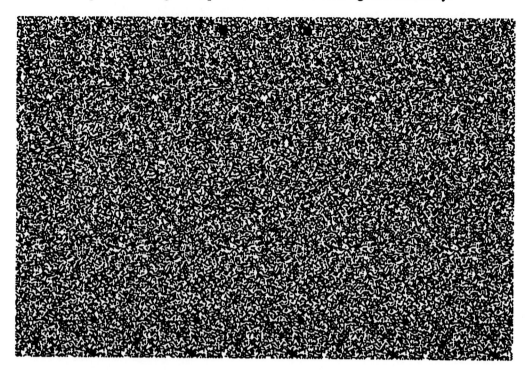

How much did the guitar cost? _____

1 - 9. Student exercise: How well did you understand the first dialogue?
Answer the following questions with **true** (T) or **false** (F). Circle the
correct answer.

1.   Hobbyman is from the planet Earth.   (T) or (F)

2.   Hobbyman hitch-hiked to Earth.   (T) or (F)

3.   There are many hobbies on Hobbyman's planet.   (T) or (F)

4.   Hobbyman came to Earth because he wanted to learn about   (T) or (F)
     hobbies.

5.   The guitarist's name is Jimmy.   (T) or (F)

6.   An electric bass guitar has 6 strings.   (T) or (F)

7.   The guitarist is now 28 years old.   (T) or (F)

8.   The guitarist started playing guitar 10 years ago.   (T) or (F)

9.   Hobbyman doesn't like the guitar very much.   (T) or (F)

10.   Hobbyman has a coffee before he leaves.   (T) or (F)

NOTES:

DID YOU KNOW THAT ...
Did you know that surfing first began in Hawaii more than 100 years ago. At that time, native Hawaiians used heavy long boards made of wood. They were about 3 or more metres long. These days, the most popular boards are called *thrusters* - short boards less than 2 metres long with 3 fins. Long boards are still popular with some surfers. All boards are very light now and are made of foam and fibreglass. Surfing became popular in the US in the 50s.

2: SURFING

LESSON FOCUS: the question word "WHAT"

♫◉⋇

2 - 1. Dialogue: Hobbyman meets a surfer.

1	**Hobbyman:**	Hi!
2	**Surfer:**	Hey dude! <u>What's happening?</u>[1]
3	**Hobbyman:**	Not much. <u>What about you?</u>[2]
4	**Surfer:**	Nothing special.
5	**Hobbyman:**	Excuse me, but <u>what are you doing?</u>[3]
6	**Surfer:**	<u>What?</u>[4]
7	**Hobbyman:**	I said, "What are you doing?"
8	**Surfer:**	I'm waxing my surfboard.
9	**Hobbyman:**	<u>What for?</u>[5]
10	**Surfer:**	<u>Say what?</u>[6]
11	**Hobbyman:**	I said, "What for?"
12	**Surfer:**	Well, I can't stand on the board if there's no wax. Too slippery! Anyway, what's your name?
13	**Hobbyman:**	I'm Hobbyman, and I'm from the planet *Nohobby*.
14	**Surfer:**	Yeah? I'm Shaun. <u>What brings you to Earth?</u>[7]
15	**Hobbyman:**	I'm visiting Earth to learn about different hobbies.
16	**Surfer:**	Cool! <u>What do you think of surfing?</u>[8]
17	**Hobbyman:**	Surfing? <u>What do you mean by "surfing"?</u>[9]
18	**Surfer:**	Surfing means riding on a board. I'm a surfer. I go to the beach, paddle my surfboard into the sea, and ride back on a wave. . . . OUCH!
19	**Hobbyman:**	<u>What's wrong?</u>[10]
20	**Surfer:**	I dropped my wax on my foot. Ouch!
21	**Hobbyman:**	Well . . . surfing sounds like a really cool hobby. Thanks for telling me all about it. Anyway Shaun, I have to go now. See ya'.
22	**Surfer:**	Okay. Catch you later, Hobbyman.

2 - 2. Short Dialogues: More "**what**" sentences.

A: What's happening, Bill?
B: Nothing much, Ted.
     What about you?
A: Not much, Bill.

     *   *   *

A: What are you doing, Greg?
B: I'm practicing my golf swing.

     *   *   *

A: What took you to Egypt?
B: What? I can't hear you!
A: I said, "What took you to Egypt?"
B: I wanted to see the pyramids.

     *   *   *

A: What if it rains tomorrow?
B: Say what?
A: I said, "What if it rains?"
B: If it rains, we'll cancel the party.

     *   *   *

A: I'm going to Tokyo next week.
B: What for?
A: I have to go to a meeting.

     *   *   *

A: What about a coffee, Bob?
B: Yes please. I'd love one.
A: What about you, Carol?
C: Yeah, thanks a lot Alice.

     *   *   *

A: What's wrong, Jack?
B: I feel sick, Jill.
A: Yeah? What's the problem?
B: I've got a headache.

     *   *   *

A: What's up, Bo?
B: I've lost all of my sheep.

     *   *   *

A: What do you think of Japan?
B: I think it's a nice country.
     What about you?
A: I think it's too expensive!

     *   *   *

A: Do you like ping pong?
B: What do you mean by
     "ping pong"?
A: Ping pong means table tennis.

     *   *   *

A: What are those black shoes
     made of?
B: They're made of leather.

     *   *   *

A: Do you like Russia, Boris?
B: Yes, I do.
A: What about America?
B: Not really.

     *   *   *

2 - 3. New Vocabulary: Do you know these words?

Bucks:	**Bucks** means *dollars*, so **ten bucks** means *ten dollars*.
Cool:	**Cool** means *interesting* or *exciting*. It's a trendy word.
Dude:	**Dude** means *man* or *guy*. **Hey dude** is a *cool* greeting.
Paddle:	**Paddling** means *lying on a surfboard and using our arms to "swim" with the board.*
Slippery:	If we **slip** easily, the ground is **slippery**.
Waxing:	**Waxing** means *rubbing wax onto the surfboard*. Of course, we can also **wax** a car, to make it shiny.

2 - 4. Language Notes:

What's happening?[1]
What's happening is a fairly common (American) greeting. It is similar to **How' you doing** or **How' you going** etc (*See 1 - 4 - 1 Language Notes*). The answers are quite limited, however. Look at the following:

Greeting	You can say:	You <u>can't</u> say:
What's happening? (Also **What's up?**)	Not much. Nothing much. Nothing special.	~~Good, thanks.~~ ~~I'm fine thanks.~~ ~~I'm okay.~~

What about you?[2]
What about you is the same as **How about you**, (*See 1-4-3 Language Notes*). **What about you** means *And you?*. **What about golf** means *And golf?* Look at the following examples:

A:	How's everything?		A:	Do you like tennis?
B:	Okay. **What about you?**		B:	Sure.
A:	I'm okay thanks.		A:	**What about golf?**
			B:	Yeah, I like golf too.

What are you doing?[3]
This is the basic **What** question. We can use it with any verb. Explanation should not be necessary. Look at the following basic examples:

What are you doing?	→ I'm waxing my surfboard.
What did you buy?	→ I bought a new computer.
What time are you leaving?	→ I'm leaving at about seven.
What school do you go to?	→ I go to Tokyo University.

What?[4]

If somebody speaks to you and you can't hear them, you can say **What**? This is *not* very polite, but it *is* common. Look at the following diagram to see some more polite examples:

Casual (Not so polite)	More polite
What? ⟶	I beg your pardon? Could you repeat that please? Once more, please? I'm sorry. What did you say? I didn't catch what you said. Pardon me? Excuse me?

What for?[5]

What for means *Why*. Compare this with **How come** (*See 1-4-4 Language Notes*). **What for** can only be used where the previous sentence was *positive*, or did not contain the word *NOT*. Look at the following diagram:

This example is good.	This example is bad.
A: I'm going to Africa. B: **What for?** A: I want to see a lion.	A: I will <u>not</u> buy a new car. B: **What for?** A: I lost all my money!

This sentence contains *not*, so we cannot use **What for**.

Why or **How come** is better here.

If we want to make a longer question, we have to divide the 2 words **What** and **for**. The question then becomes **What . . . . for**? Look at the following examples:

Good question ⟶	Bad question ⟶	Good question
Why is he going?	**What for** is he going?	**What** is he going **for**?
Why did you come?	**What for** did you come?	**What** did you come **for**?
Why was she here?	**What for** was she here?	**What** was she here **for**?

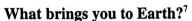

Say what?[6]

Say what is the same as **What**? (*See Language Note 4, this lesson*). **Say what** is very casual American slang. Some people never use this expression - some people use it very often.

What brings you to Earth?[7]

What brings you to ... (or **What brought you ...**) is the same as *Why did you come to ...?*. The expression **What took you to ...** is the same as *Why did you go to ... ?*. The expression **What takes you to ...** is the same as *Why are you going to ... ?*. Look at the following:

Why did you come here?	**What brings you here?** **What brought you here?**
Why did you go to her house? ⟶	**What took you to her house?**
Why are you going to Africa? ⟶	**What takes you to Africa?**

What do you think of surfing?[8]

We can ask peoples opinions by saying **What do you think of ... ?** We can also say **What do you think about ... ?** This is similar to *How do you like . .* (*See 1 - 4 - 9 Language Notes*). We can answer in many ways. Look at the following examples:

What do you think of tennis? **What do you think about tennis?**	I think tennis is really good. *or* I don't like tennis. *or* Tennis is a boring game. *or* It's okay, I guess.

What do you mean by "surfing"?[9]

If you don't understand a word, you can say **What do you mean by. .** You can also say **What does ... mean?** Look at the example:

What do you mean by *slam dunk*?	*Slam dunk* **means** jumping high in the air, and throwing the ball down through the basket.

What's wrong?[10]

If somebody has a problem, we often say **What's wrong?** There are many other expressions which have the same meaning. Look at the following:

| What's wrong? | What's the problem? | What's the matter? |
| What's up? | What's the trouble? | What happened? |

♫☺🎥

2 - 5. Student Exercises: Fill in the blanks. Choose the best sentence from the list on this page.

Shaun & Rabbit are 2 surfers. They meet in Shaun's surf shop.

1 **Shaun:** ⬚
2 **Rabbit:** Not much. ⬚
3 **Shaun:** Nothing. Anyway, ⬚
4 **Rabbit:** I want to buy a new board.
5 **Shaun:** ⬚ ⬚
6 **Rabbit:** My old one's broken.
7 **Shaun:** Okay. ⬚
8 **Rabbit:** Too short. I need a longer one.
9 **Shaun:** Sure. ⬚
10 **Rabbit:** ⬚
11 **Shaun:** This board costs six hundred bucks.
12 **Rabbit:** ⬚
13 **Shaun:** I said, "This surfboard costs six hundred bucks".
14 **Rabbit:** ⬚
15 **Shaun:** "Bucks" means dollars.
16 **Rabbit:** Wow! Too expensive! I'll use my old board.

Choose the best sentences for the blanks.
a) Say what?
b) What is the price?
c) What about this one?
d) What for?
e) What brings you here today, Rabbit?
f) What's happening Rabbit?
g) What do you mean by "bucks"?
h) What about you, Shaun?
i) What do you think of this board?
j) What's wrong with your old board?

2 - 6. Student Exercise: Select the best answer.

1. If somebody says **What's happening?**, a good answer is:
    (a) I'm fine, thanks.   (b) Nothing much.
    (c) Okay, thank you.   (d) Not bad.

2. **What about you?** is the same as:
    (a) What of you?   (b) What about me?
    (c) How about you?   (d) What are you?

3.	Which expression is NOT the same as **What?**
	(a)	I beg your pardon?	(b)	Once more, please.
	(c)	Are you speaking?	(d)	I'm sorry. What did you say?

4. 	**What for?** is the same as:
	(a)	Who for?	(b)	Where for?
	(c)	Which for?	(d)	Why?

5.	If somebody says **Say what?**, he means:
	(a)	Pardon me?	(b)	Please say the word "What".
	(c)	What time is it now?	(d)	Why?

6.	**What brings you here?** means:
	(a)	How did you come here?	(b)	Why did you come here?
	(c)	What are you bringing	(d)	What did you bring here?
		here?

7.	Which expression is the same as **What do you think of sushi?**.
	(a)	What about sushi?	(b)	What do you think about sushi?
	(c)	How do you think of	(d)	What are you thinking of sushi?
		sushi?

8.	**What do you mean by "surfing"?** is the same as:
	(a)	What means "surfing"?	(b)	What does "surfing" mean?
	(c)	Is "surfing" mean?	(d)	"Surfing" is mean, what?

9.	Which of the following is not the same as **What's wrong?**
	(a)	What's the matter?	(b)	What's the problem?
	(c)	What's the trouble?	(d)	What's the bad?

10.	**Surfing is cool** means:
	(a)	Surfing is very cold.	(b)	Surfing is interesting and exciting.
	(c)	Surfing is boring.	(d)	Surfers are not very friendly.

2 - 7.	Review of this lesson's major points. Do you understand these questions
	and expressions?

What's happening?	What's wrong?
What about you?	What do you mean by "surfing"?
What?	What do you think of surfing?
What for?	What took you to Egypt?
Say what?	What if it rains tomorrow?
What about a coffee?	What are those shoes made of?
What's up?	What brings you here?

2 - 8. Student Exercise: STEREOGRAM. Can you see the hidden answer?

Rabbit: Hey Shaun. What's happening, man?
Shaun: Say what?
Rabbit: I said, "What's happening?"
Shaun: Not much, Rabbit. What about you?
Rabbit: Nothing much. Umm, can I borrow ten bucks?
Shaun: What for?
Rabbit: I want to buy a new (. . . . .).

What does Rabbit want to buy? To find out, please look at the stereogram.

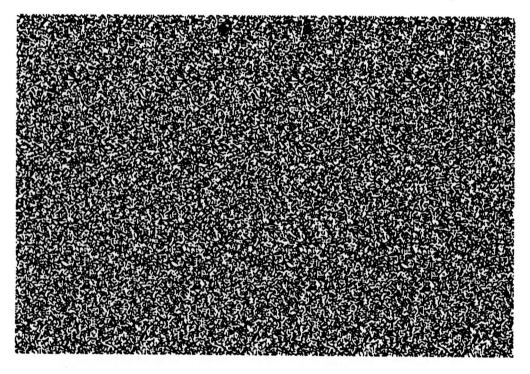

What does Rabbit want to buy? _____

2 - 9. Student exercise: How well did you understand the first dialogue?
Answer the following questions with **true** (T) or **false** (F). Circle the
correct answer.

1.   The surfer is waxing his surfboard.   (T) or (F)

2.   It is easy to stand on a surfboard if there is no wax.   (T) or (F)

3.   The surfer's name is Björn.   (T) or (F)

4.   Hobbyman thinks surfing is a really cool hobby.   (T) or (F)

5.   The surfer paddles his surfboard into the sea, and rides   (T) or (F)
     back on wives.

6.   Hobbyman dropped some wax on his foot.   (T) or (F)

7.   At first, Hobbyman doesn't understand the word "surfing".   (T) or (F)

8.   The board is too slippery if there is too much wax.   (T) or (F)

9.   The surfer is only twenty one years old.   (T) or (F)

10. Surfing began in Hawaii more than 100 years ago.   (T) or (F)

NOTES:

DID YOU KNOW THAT...

Did you know that playing cards are more than 600 years old. In 1392, a French painter designed and painted 52 cards. The 52 cards were divided into 4 suits - spades, clubs, diamonds and hearts. Spades represented soldiers, clubs represented farmers, diamonds represented artists (they often wore diamond shaped hats) and hearts represented religion. Nowadays, cards is the most popular game in the world!

3: CARDS

LESSON FOCUS: the verb "TAKE"

♫◉🎥

3 - 1. Dialogue: Hobbyman meets a card player.

1 **Hobbyman:**   Hi!

2 **Card Player:** Hi! You're Hobbyman, right? I'm Brick. I read about you in the newspapers. Oh - please take a seat.[1]

3 **Hobbyman:**   Thanks. Ah - what are these?

4 **Card Player:** They're cards. I love playing cards!

5 **Hobbyman:**   Cards? Do you play by yourself?

6 **Card Player:** Of course not! We're taking a break now.[2] We played all night. Simon's taking a shower,[3] John's taking a walk[4] and Glenn's taking a pee.[5]

7 **Hobbyman:**   You played all night? Do you take off any time for dinner?[6]

8 **Card Player:** Oh yeah. We usually take 5 or 10 minutes[7] and eat some take-away food.

9 **Hobbyman:**   What games do you play?

10 **Card Player:** Well, if we gamble, we usually play poker. Hey, take a look at this[8] - four aces and a king - pretty good, eh?

11 **Hobbyman:**   You gamble? You bet money?

12 **Card Player:** Sure. Take it easy, Hobbyman![9] We only play for small money.

13 **Hobbyman:**   When did you start gambling?

14 **Card Player:** Well, I first took part in a game 10 years ago.[10] My father took me to Las Vegas.[11] We drove and it took over 10 hours![12] We played Black Jack and we took home $2000.[13]

15 **Hobbyman:**   Your father took you to Vegas?

16 **Card Player:** Yeah. He was a real gambler. I take after him.[14] Actually, my mother couldn't take his gambling.[15] She left him.

17 **Hobbyman:**   Well thanks for talking to me, Brick. I'm sorry I took up your time.[16]

18 **Card Player:** No problem, Hobbyman. Take care![17]

19 **Hobbyman:**   Okay Brick. See you later.

3 - 2. Short Dialogues: More **"take"** sentences.

A: I'm tired.
B: Okay. Let's take a break!°

*   *   *

A: Gee, you smell bad, Glenn!
B: Sorry! I'll take a bath.°

*   *   *

A: I've been really busy recently!
B: Why don't you take a day off?°
A: That's a good idea.

*   *   *

A: I'm going to take a walk.°
See ya' later.
B: Okay. Take care.

*   *   *

A: Wow! Take a look° at that girl!
B: Yeah. She's beautiful, isn't she?

*   *   *

A: When are you taking your winter°
vacation?
B: My boss said I can't take any
more time off.°

*   *   *

A: Please take a seat.°
B: Thankyou very much.

*   *   *

A: Do you take sugar° in your coffee?
B: Yes - 3 spoons please.

*   *   *

A: What can I do? Help me!
B: Hey! Take it easy, O.J.!

*   *   *

A: Where did you go last week?
B: Dad took me to Disneyland!

*   *   *

A: Are you taking part in the
game?
B: I wish I could but I'm busy.

*   *   *

A: I've got a bad headache.
B: Go to bed and take some
medicine.

*   *   *

A: You're just like your Mum.
B: Yeah. I take after her.

*   *   *

A: Why did you quit your job?
B: Well, everyday I worked
from 6am to 9pm. I just
couldn't take it any more!

*   *   *

A: How long did it take?
B: It took over 6 hours!

*   *   *

A: Anyway, I have to go now.
B: Okay. Take care. 'Bye!

*   *   *

3 - 3. New Vocabulary: Do you know these words?

Cards: **Cards** are also called **playing cards**.
Dad: **Dad** is the short form of **Father**.
Gamble: **Gamble** means *betting* or *playing games for money*.
Gambler: A **gambler** is a person who **gambles**.
Mum: **Mum** is the short form of **Mother**.
Take-away: **Take-away** or **take-away food** means *buying food from a shop or restaurant and eating it somewhere else.* (In American English, **take out** is more popular).
Vacation: **Vacation** is the same as *holiday*.

3 - 4. **Language Notes:** Language Notes:

This lesson focuses on the word **take**. **Take** has many meanings. In language notes 1 to 8, *have* can be used instead of **take**. The meaning is the same. In Short Dialogues 3 - 2, *have* can be used instead of **take** if there is a ° mark.

TAKE	HAVE	MEANING
Take a seat.[1]	Have a seat	Take a seat = Sit down.
We're taking a break now.[2]	We're having a break now.	Take a break = Rest or relax for a short time.
Simon's taking a shower.[3]	Simon's having a shower.	Take a shower = to wash in a shower.
John's taking a walk.[4]	John's having a walk.	Take a walk = Go for a walk.
Glenn's taking a pee.[5] *(Instead of "pee", we can use the word "piss", but "piss" is slang and not very polite.)*	Glenn's having a pee.	Take a pee = Go to the toilet; urinate
Do you take off any time for dinner?[6]	Do you have off any time for dinner?	Take off time = Rest or relax.
We usually take 5 or 10 minutes.[7]	We usually have 5 or 10 minutes.	Take 5 = Rest or relax for a short time.
Take a look at this![8]	Have a look at this!	Take a look = look at.
OTHERS		
Do you take milk in your tea?	Do you have milk in your tea?	Take milk = Put milk in your drink.
Let's take a bath!	Let's have a bath!	Take a bath = To bath.

Take it easy, Hobbyman![9]

Take it easy means *Relax* or *Don't worry*. This is very conversational English, and is very common.

I first took part in a game 10 years ago.[10]

Take part in means *participate*, *join in* or *play*, (in the case of games and sports).

> I **took part in** the celebration.
> Did your daughter **take part in** the speech competition?
> Is your team **taking part in** the tournament?

My father took me to Las Vegas.[11]

Take means to *carry*, or *"go with" a person, an animal or an object from one place* (near the speaker) *to another place* (far from the speaker). **Take** is the opposite of **bring**. Look at the following examples:

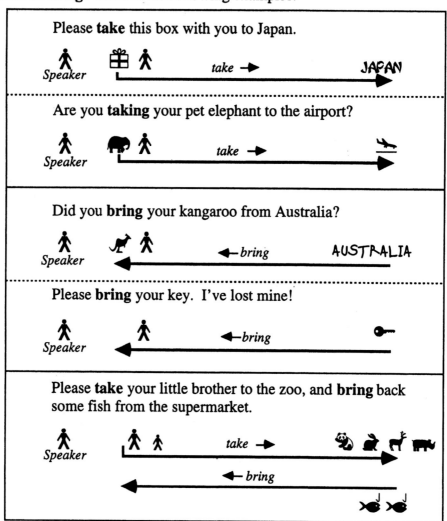

Please **take** this box with you to Japan.

Speaker — take → JAPAN

Are you **taking** your pet elephant to the airport?

Speaker — take →

Did you **bring** your kangaroo from Australia?

Speaker ← bring — AUSTRALIA

Please **bring** your key. I've lost mine!

Speaker ← bring

Please **take** your little brother to the zoo, and **bring** back some fish from the supermarket.

Speaker — take → ← bring

As you can see, **take** moves away from the speaker; **bring** moves towards the speaker.

It took over 10 hours![12]
Take is often used with time. For example:

> From Tokyo to Sydney by plane **takes** 9 hours.
> It only **takes** 1 season to become a good snowboarder.

We took home $2000.[13]
Take home or **bring home** means *to carry home*. (*See page 28 Language Note 3-4-11 again.*)

I take after him.[14]
Take after means *look like* or *be like*. If a young boy *looks like* his father, we can say that **He takes after his father**. If a girl has the *same* personality as her mother, we can say that *She takes after her mother*.

My mother couldn't take his gambling.[15]
Can't take means *can't stand* or *can't endure*. **Can take** means *can endure*. Look at the following examples:

> Every day he played his drums from 9pm to 1am. It was too noisy. **I couldn't take it**, so I moved to a different house.
>
> I'm joining the army next year. I heard it's very tough, but I think **I can take it**.

I'm sorry I took up your time.[16]
Take up is often used with time. It is similar to **take** in *Language Note 3-4-12* (See above). The expression **I'm sorry I took up your time** is often used to finish a (business) conversation: It is not used between friends.

Take care![17]
When we say **Goodbye** to a friend, we often also say **Take care of yourself** or **Take care**. This means *Be careful and don't do anything dangerous*. This greeting is very common.

Take[18]
Take can also mean *Steal*. **He took my bike** means *He stole my bike*.

♫●🎥

3 - 5. Student Exercises: Fill in the blanks.
Choose the best sentence from the list below.

1	**Mr Trump:**	Let's have a game of cards!
2	**Mrs Trump:**	Not now, Donald. [ ]
3	**Mr Trump:**	Okay. How about after you come back?
4	**Mrs Trump:**	No thanks. [ ]
5	**Mr Trump:**	Well, let's have a short game now.
6	**Mrs Trump:**	No! I don't like playing with you. You always win! [ ]
7	**Mr Trump:**	Hey! [ ] I like winning!
8	**Mrs Trump:**	Your father also liked winning. [ ]
9	**Mr Trump:**	Yeah - I'm just like my father. [ ]
10	**Mrs Trump:**	Outside?
11	**Mr Trump:**	Yeah. [ ]
12	**Mrs Trump:**	Wow! [ ]

Choose the best sentences for the blanks.

a) I can't take it!

b) We'd better not take a swim!

c) You take after him.

d) I have to take the dog for a walk.

e) Walking the dog takes a long time.

f) Hey - take a look outside!

g) Take it easy!

h) Your dog's taking a pee in the swimming pool!

3 - 6. Student Exercise: Select the best answer.

1. **Please take a seat** means:
(a) Please steal this seat.
(b) Please move this seat.
(c) Please seat.
(d) Please sit down.

2. **Take it easy** means:
(a) Don't worry!
(b) It is easy.
(c) Don't take it!
(d) It is easy to take.

3. **I participated in the game** or **I joined in the game** is the same as:
(a) I took over the game.
(b) I took part in the game.
(c) I can't take the game.
(d) I took the game.

4. If you like black coffee, you should say:
(a) I don't take milk in my coffee.
(b) I don't take up milk in my coffee.
(c) I don't take by milk in my coffee.
(d) I don't take after milk in my coffee.

5. **Janet is like Michael** is the same as:
   (a) Janet takes over Michael. (b) Janet takes after Michael.
   (c) Janet takes up Michael. (d) Janet is Michael.

6. When we say goodbye to somebody, we often also say
   (a) Take after yourself! (b) Take cars!
   (c) Take care! (d) Take over!

7. **He couldn't take her singing** means:
   (a) He could not stand her (b) He liked her singing very
        singing.   much.
   (c) She could sing better (d) She only sang Janet Jackson
        than him.   songs.

8. John lives in New York. Yoko lives in Tokyo. John buys a present for
   Yoko in New York. He goes to Tokyo and gives the present to Yoko.
   What does he say?
   (a) I took this present from (b) I brought this present from New
        New York.   York.
   (c) I take this present from (d) I bring this present from New
        New York.   York.

9. Michael went to the movies by himself. His sister wanted to go, but
   Michael refused. After the movie, Michael went home. His mother
   was angry. She said:
   (a) Why didn't you bring (b) Why didn't you take your sister
        your sister to the movies?   to the movies?
   (c) Why did you bring your (d) Why did you take your sister to
        sister to the movies?   the movies?

10. A **gambler** is a person who:
    (a) likes playing cards. (b) smokes a lot.
    (c) lives in New York. (d) plays games for money.

3 - 7. Review of this lesson's major points. Do you understand these expressions?

Take a seat	Take it easy!	Take care.
Take a break	Take part in	Take up (time)
Take a shower	I took him to Japan.	Can take it
Take a walk	I brought her here.	Can't take it
Take a pee	It takes 10 hours.	Take after
Take off time	Take home	Take (Medicine)
Take a look	Do you take milk?	Take (Steal)

3 - 8. Student Exercise: STEREOGRAM. Can you see the hidden answer?

Hobbyman:	Why are you in jail?
Ronald:	I took some money from a bank.
Hobbyman:	Why?
Ronald:	Well . . . I took some drugs and I became kind of crazy.
Hobbyman:	Did any of your friends take part in the robbery?
Ronald:	No. I did it alone.
Hobbyman:	And how much money did you take?
Ronald:	Ah . . . I took (. . . . .).

To find how much money Ronald took, please look at the stereogram carefully.

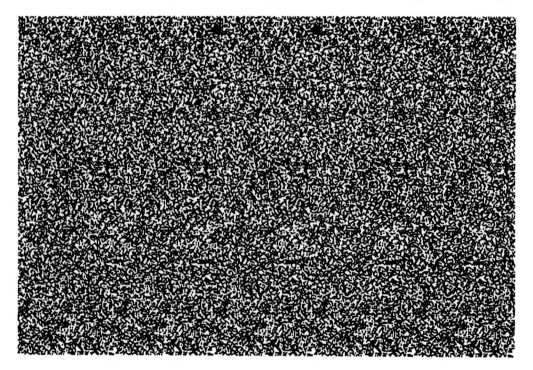

How much money did Ronald take from the bank? _____

3 - 9. Student exercise: How well did you understand the first dialogue? Answer the following questions with **true** (T) or **false** (F). Circle the correct answer.

1. Brick doesn't like playing cards. (T) or (F)

2. Simon's taking a walk. (T) or (F)

3.   John's taking a pee.   (T) or (F)

4.   Brick has four aces and a queen.   (T) or (F)

5.   Brick first took part in a game 15 years ago.   (T) or (F)

6.   Brick doesn't take after his father.   (T) or (F)

7.   Brick won $2000 playing poker.   (T) or (F)

8.   Brick saw Hobbyman on TV.   (T) or (F)

9.   Brick has never been to Las Vegas.   (T) or (F)

10.   Playing cards are less tham 600 years old.   (T) or (F)

NOTES:

DID YOU KNOW THAT ...

Did you know that making your own beer is very common in many foreign countries. There are many reasons why people brew their own beer. First, it is very cheap! 25 litres costs about US $10. Also, making your own beer is very satisfying. Ingredients are very cheap and are often available in supermarkets. You can even change the flavour by adding your favourite tea, spice or fruit! Cheers!!

4: BEERMAKING

LESSON FOCUS: the verb "HAVE"

♪☺📷

4 - 1. Dialogue: Hobbyman meets a home-brewer.

1	**Hobbyman:**	Hello
2	**Brewer:**	Ow . . . Ouch . . . Good morning . . . Ow!
3	**Hobbyman:**	What's the matter?
4	**Brewer:**	I have a bad hangover.[1] Anyway, who are you?
5	**Hobbyman:**	I'm Hobbyman. I'm from the planet *Nohobby* and I came to Earth to learn about hobbies.
6	**Brewer:**	Yeah? I have a nice hobby.[2] I make my own beer. Sometimes I drink too much.
7	**Hobbyman:**	Why do you have a red face?[3]
8	**Brewer:**	'Because I drank too much. Last night I had a meeting[4] with my beer making friends. We had too much to drink.[5]
9	**Hobbyman:**	Did you enjoy yourself?
10	**Brewer:**	Oh, I had a really good time, thanks.[6]
11	**Hobbyman:**	How many different beers do you have?[7]
12	**Brewer:**	I have over 10 different beers and stouts. If I have a cold,[8] I drink this stout. If I have a fight with my wife[8], I drink lots of this lager.
13	**Hobbyman:**	You have a wife?[9]
14	**Brewer:**	Yeah. I have a wife and 3 kids. I also have a dog.[10]
15	**Hobbyman:**	How old are your kids?
16	**Brewer:**	They are 7, 5 and 1 month. My wife had a baby last month.[11] Ah . . . Do you have a light?[12]
17	**Hobbyman:**	Sorry, I don't smoke. You said you had more than 10 different beers. Which is your favourite?
18	**Brewer:**	Hmmm . . . I have no idea.[13] They all taste good to me.
19	**Hobbyman:**	Okay. I don't have anymore questions. Thanks and good-bye.

4 - 2. Short Dialogues: More "**have**" sentences.

A: What's wrong, Bill?
B: I've got a bad headache.

*   *   *

A: We're having a party, tomorrow.
B: We had a party last week.

*   *   *

A: How many wives do you have, Mahommad?
B: I've got twenty. How about you?
A: I only have one.

*   *   *

A: Do you have any pets, Mic?
B: Yeah. I've got a pet crocodile. What about you, Basil?
A: I've got a dog and several gold-fish.

*   *   *

A: Are you hungry?
B: No. I just had something to eat.

*   *   *

A: Did you drink much last night?
B: Yeah. I sure had a lot to drink!

*   *   *

A: Hey, Woody, 'you got a light?
B: Sure. Here you are.
A: And do you have a cigarette?
B: Yeah.

*   *   *

A: Ringo has a really big nose.
B: And George has long hair.

*   *   *

A: How was the party?
B: We had a great time, thanks.

*   *   *

A: My wife had another baby!
B: Congratulations! How many kids do you have now, Fred?
A: Now, I have three sons.

*   *   *

A: What's wrong?
B: I had a really bad day today. I had a fight with my wife, an argument with my boss and my son had a car accident.

*   *   *

A: When did John Lennon die?
B: I have no idea!

*   *   *

A: Do you have any time, today?
B: No, sorry. I'm busy all day.

*   *   *

A: 'You got the time?
B: Eh? I've got bad hearing.
A: I said, "Do you have the time?
B: Sure. It's one thirty.

*   *   *

4 - 3. New Vocabulary: Do you know these words?

Brewer: A **brewer** is a man who makes beer.
Hangover: If you drink too much, the next day you will have a **hangover**.
Kids: **Kids** means *children*.
Lager: **Lager** is a type of beer.
Ow: If we experience pain, we usually say **ow** or **ouch**. (Pronunciation
               is the same as *ow* in *how* or *cow*.)
Stout: **Stout** is the same as *black beer*.

4 - 4. Language Notes: Language Notes

<u>I have a bad hangover.</u>[1] **<u>Why do you have a red face?</u>**[3] **<u>If I have a cold . . .</u>**[8]
When we talk about our body, sickness or health, we often use the word **have**.
In conversation, we often say **have got** instead of **have**. The meaning of both is
the same. (*We only use **have got** in present tense.*) Look at the following
examples:

I **have** a bad hangover.	⟶ I've got a bad hangover.
Why do you **have** a red face?	⟶ Why **have** you **got** a red face?
Freddy **has** AIDS.	⟶ Freddy **has got** AIDS.
Does Ringo **have** a big nose?	⟶ **Has** Ringo **got** a big nose?
You **have** a temperature.	⟶ **You've got** a temperature.

We can also say that a cold, fever, headache, or hangover (etc) is *bad*. This
means that our body condition is *bad*. The opposite of *bad* is *slight*.

<u>I have a nice hobby.</u>[2]   **<u>How many different beers do you have?</u>**[7]
This **have** refers to ownership. It is very common. Look at the following
examples:

He **has** two cars.
You **have** a very nice house.
We **have** no money.
I **have** two jobs, so I'm always busy.
How many CD's **have** you **got**?

We *can* use **have got** instead of **have** in this case.

<u>Last night I had a meeting.</u>[4]
We use the word **have** when many people gather together. Look at the
following examples:

> John **had** *a party* last night.
> We **have** *a meeting* every Tuesday.
> I **have** *my tennis lesson* on Friday.
> They **had** *their wedding reception* in Hawaii.

We can also use **have** with other words, such as *barbecue, party, funeral, meeting, conference, convention, re-union, lesson, wedding reception* or *any gathering of people*.
We *can't* use **have got** instead of **have** in this case.

We had too much to drink.[5]

The word **have** is often used with eating and drinking. Look at the following examples:

> Could I **have something to drink?**   She **had something to eat**.
> I want to **have a drink**.   I **had two pies** for lunch.
> How many **beers** did you **have?**   What did you **have** for dinner?

We *can't* use **have got** instead of **have** in this case.

I had a really good time, thanks.[6]

Have a good time is the same as *enjoy oneself*. Look at the following:

> She **had a** *good* **time**. → She *enjoyed herself*.
> Dale **had a** *bad* **time**. → Dale *didn't enjoy himself*.

We *can't* use **have got** instead of **have** in this case.

If I have a fight with my wife . . .[8]   My wife had a baby last month.[11]

Have is a very useful verb. If you are not sure what verb to use, try using **have**. Look at some of the uses of the verb **have**:

> We **had a fight**.   My sister just **had a baby!**
> He **had a love affair!**   **Have a nice day!**
> Did you **have an accident?**   He **had an argument** with her.
> I **had a dream**.   She **had a heart attack**.

In most of these cases, we *can't* use **have got** instead of **have**.

You have a wife?[9]

We use the word **have** for family members and friends etc. For example,
I *have* **a beautiful wife and son. I also** *have* **lots of friends, so I'm happy.**
We *can* use **have got** instead of **have** in this case. (*But only present tense.*)

I also have a dog.[10]

We also use the word **have** for pets and animals. For example,
She *has* 2 dogs, a cat and some goldfish. I don't *have* any pets.
We *can* use **have got** instead of **have** in this case. (*But only present tense.*)

Do you have a light?[12]/ I have no idea.[13]

Some **have** sentences are very common in *slang* daily conversation. Look at the following examples:

Grammatical	More Conversational	Shorter slang form
Do you **have** a light? *light* means *lighter.*	**Have** you **got** a light?	**'Got** a light?
Do you **have** a smoke? *smoke* means *cigarette.*	**Have** you **got** a smoke?	**'Got** a smoke?
Do you **have** the time? *Do you have the time*	**Have** you **got** the time? means *What time is it ?*	'You **got** the time?
I **have** no idea! *I have no idea* means	**I've got** no idea! *I don't know.*	'No idea!

¤Remember: **Have you got any/some time** and **Have you got the time** are different.

Question	Meaning
Have you got *any time*? Have you got *some time*? Do you have *any time*? Do you have *some time*? →	Do you have some free time? I want to talk to you. etc.
Have you got *the time*? Do you have *the time*? →	What time is it now?

4 - 5. Student Exercises: Fill in the blanks.
Choose the best sentence from the list on the next page.

1	**Bud:**	Hi Mr Miller. You don't look well. [⬚]
2	**Mr Miller:**	No Bud. [⬚]
3	**Bud:**	And you drank too much?
4	**Mr Miller:**	[⬚]
5	**Bud:**	How much did you drink?
6	**Mr Miller:**	[⬚]
7	**Bud:**	Did you enjoy yourself at the party?
8	**Mr Miller:**	Yeah. [⬚] Anyway, how's your wife?
9	**Bud:**	She's good, thanks. [⬚]
10	**Mr Miller:**	Congratulations! [⬚]
11	**Bud:**	Why?
12	**Mr Miller:**	[⬚]

Choose the best sentences for the blanks.

a) I had a really good time.   e) Because I haven't got a wife!
b) I don't have any kids.   f) Have you got a cold?
c) Last night I had an office party. g) Yeah, I really had a lot to drink.
d) We had another baby last week. h) I had 10 or 11 beers and 4 or 5 stouts.

4 - 6. Student Exercise: Select the best answer.

1. If you drink too much and your head hurts, you can say:
    (a) I am a hangover.   (b) It is a hangover.
    (c) I have hungover.   (d) I have a hangover.

2. Which of the following sentences is NOT good?
    (a) We have a meeting every Friday.   (b) She has a singing lesson twice a week.
    (c) I have a guitar every Sunday.   (d) We had our wedding in Hawaii.

3. Instead of saying **We enjoyed ourselves**, we can say:
    (a) We had an enjoy time.   (b) We had a good time.
    (c) We timed ourselves.   (d) We had enjoyment.

4. Which of the following sentences is NOT good. (Hint: food)
    (a) I'll have a beer, please.   (b) We didn't have anything to eat.
    (c) Could I have 2 meat pies. (d) All sentences are okay.

5. Which of the following sentences is NOT good?
    (a) Rosemary had a baby.   (b) She is having a fight with him.
    (c) O.J. had a bad day.   (d) All sentences are okay.

6. Which of the following sentences is NOT good? (Hint: Family)
    (a) You don't have any grand-parents?   (b) He hasn't got any pets in his house.
    (c) I had many friends at high school.   (d) All sentences are okay.

7. You want to borrow somebody's cigarette lighter. Which of the following sentences is NOT good.
    (a) 'You got a light?   (b) May I borrow your lighter?
    (c) Do you have a lighter? (d) Are you alight?

8. Instead of saying **I don't know**, we can say:
    (a) I don't understand.   (b) I have know idea.
    (c) No idea.   (d) I don't no idea.

9.   A person who makes beer is called:
      (a)   a beer-man.   (b)   a brewer.
      (c)   a making beer person.   (d)   a barrel.

10.   Instead of saying **black beer**, we can say:
      (a)   stoat.   (b)   grope.
      (c)   grout.   (d)   stout.

4 - 7. Review of this lesson's major points. Do you understand these sentences?

I have a bad hangover.   I had a fight with my wife.
I have a nice hobby.   I also have a dog.
I had a meeting last night.   My wife had a baby last week.
I had too much to drink.   'You got a light?
I had a really good time.   I have no idea.
Why do you have a red face?   Do you have any time?
I've got bad hearing.   'You got the time?

4 - 8. Student Exercise: Can you help Hobbyman?
        Hobbyman wants to drink some home-brew beer. Can you help him get
        from the left side of the puzzle to the right side of the puzzle? Target time
        is **thirty seconds**.

4 - 9. Student Exercise: Below is a list of beer words. Can you find all of
them in the word search below? Words are hidden horizontally - (left to
right), vertically - (top to bottom) and diagonally - (top left to bottom
right). Target time is **two minutes**.

```
M  C  B  I  T  T  E  R  A  L  E  M
C  U  S  T  O  U  T  B  C  M  M  A
S  U  G  A  R  W  I  A  S  B  O  L
P  I  L  S  E  N  E  R  P  A  V  T
W  J  V  C  A  N  V  R  O  R  S  C
A  I  R  L  O  C  K  E  O  L  B  A
W  A  T  E  R  G  Y  L  N  E  E  P
H  C  B  O  T  T  L  E  J  Y  E  P
E  Z  N  G  L  A  S  S  A  U  R  E
A  H  O  B  B  Y  M  A  N  S  G  R
D  S  D  R  A  U  G  H  T  T  T  A
L  A  G  E  R  H  O  P  S  K  R  D
```

Airlock	Bottle	Hobbyman	Pilsener
Ale	Can	Hops	Spoon
Barley	Capper	Jug	Stout
Barrel	Draught	Lager	Sugar
Beer	Glass	Malt	Water
Bitter	Head	Mug	Yeast

4 - 10. Student exercise: How well did you understand the first dialogue?
Answer the following questions with **true** (T) or **false** (F). Circle the
correct answer.

1. The home-brewer's name is Gustav.   (T) or (F)

2. Hobbyman had too much to drink last night.   (T) or (F)

3. The home-brewer went to a meeting with his beer making   (T) or (F)
    friends last night.

4. The home-brewer has a wife, 3 kids and 2 dogs.   (T) or (F)

5. If the home-brewer has a cold, he drinks stout.   (T) ot (F)

6. The home-brewer has more than 10 different types of beer.   (T) or (F)

7. Hobbyman doesn't smoke.   (T) or (F)

8. Hobbyman has a red face.   (T) or (F)

9. The brewer's wife had a baby last month.   (T) or (F)

10. The brewer's favourite drink is lager.   (T) or (F)

NOTES:

DID YOU KNOW THAT ...

Did you know that the most popular stroke in swimming is *Overarm* (also called *the crawl* or *the Australian crawl*). *Overarm* was first used in 1862, in Manchester, England, and was invented by Harry Gardener. In 1876, swimming fins (or flippers) were also invented. Perhaps the most famous swimmer in the world was an American called *Johnny Weissmuller* (1904-1984). He won 5 Olympic Gold medals, had 67 world records and he also played *Tarzan* in many jungle adventure films.

5: SWIMMING

LESSON FOCUS: "THERE IS/ARE, TOO MANY/MUCH"
"NOT ENOUGH, LIKES/ DISLIKES"

♫◎🎥
5 - 1. Dialogue: Hobbyman meets a swimmer.

1	**Hobbyman:**	Hi!
2	**Swimmer:**	Hi! I saw you on TV! You're Hobbyman, aren't you? I'm Mark Splitz. Nice to meet you.
3	**Hobbyman:**	Good to meet you. So, <u>what do you like doing in your spare time?</u>[1]
4	**Swimmer:**	Oh, I love swimming. It's great. <u>I'm crazy about it!</u>[2]
5	**Hobbyman:**	Well, <u>there aren't any swimmers</u>[3] on Nohobby, so please tell me something about it.
6	**Swimmer:**	Sure. <u>There are 4 major strokes.</u>[4] There is *freestyle*, also called *the Australian crawl*. There is *breaststroke*, there is *backstroke* and there is *butterfly*.
7	**Hobbyman:**	<u>Aren't there any more?</u>[5]
8	**Swimmer:**	Well - there is also *sidestroke* and *dog-paddle*. *Sidestroke* is for life-saving and *dog-paddle* is for learning.
9	**Hobbyman:**	Which stroke is your favourite?
10	**Swimmer:**	I really like freestyle.
11	**Hobbyman:**	What about breaststroke?
12	**Swimmer:**	<u>It's okay,</u>[6] but <u>it's too slow.</u>[7]
13	**Hobbyman:**	How about butterfly?
14	**Swimmer:**	<u>I can't stand it.</u>[8] <u>It's too difficult!</u>[9]
15	**Hobbyman:**	What's the worst thing about swimming?
16	**Swimmer:**	<u>There are always too many people</u>[10] in the pool, and <u>it costs too much money.</u>[11]
17	**Hobbyman:**	Are there any other bad points?
18	**Swimmer:**	Yeah. <u>There aren't enough pretty girls.</u>[12]
19	**Hobbyman:**	Well, thanks for telling me about swimming. See ya' 'round.
20	**Swimmer:**	Okay Hobbyman. See you later.

5 - 2. Short Dialogues: More "**there is/are, too many/much**" sentences.

A: Are there any casino's in Australia?
B: Yeah, there are some.

*   *   *

A: Is there a God?
B: I don't know, John-Paul.

*   *   *

A: Let's play football, O.J.!
B: I can't. I'm too busy.

*   *   *

A: What do you think of America, Rodney?
B: Too many guns and too much crime.

*   *   *

A: Elvis, you eat too much!
B: Yeah, I drink too much, too.

*   *   *

A: Do you like swimming, Johnny?
B: Sure. I'm crazy about it.

*   *   *

A: Do you like sumo wrestling, Rie?
B: Sumo wrestling? I guess it's okay.

*   *   *

A: Aren't there any casino's in Japan?
B: No, there aren't any.

*   *   *

A: Isn't there a Santa Claus?
B: No, there's not.

*   *   *

A: Let's go skiing, Alberto!
B: Nah. I'm not good enough.

*   *   *

A: How do you like Japan, Boris?
B: Not enough space and not enough leisure time.

*   *   *

A: Chad, you don't eat enough!
B: I know. I'm on a diet.

*   *   *

A: Do you like raw fish, Simon?
B: No way. I can't stand it.

*   *   *

A: How do you like classical music, Ludwig?
B: Classical music is alright.

*   *   *

5 - 3. New Vocabulary: Do you know these words?

Backstroke: **Backstroke** is a style of swimming where we swim lying on our back.

Breaststroke: **Breaststroke** is a style of swimming where we swim on our front, and use a frog kick.

Butterfly: **Butterfly** is the most difficult stroke. We use a 'dolphin' kick with our legs together.

Dog-paddle: When people learn to swim, they often use **dog-paddle**. This stroke is similar to a dog swimming.

Freestyle: **Freestyle** really means any style, but in everyday conversation, **freestyle** means *overarm* swimming. This is also called *the crawl* or *the Australian crawl*.

Sidestroke: **Sidestroke** was the most popular stroke 100 years ago. The swimmer swims on his side. This is now only used for life-saving.

Stroke: **Stroke** means *swimming method*.

The crawl: See **Freestyle**.

5 - 4. Language Notes: Language Notes

What do you like doing in your spare time?[1]
Often, instead of saying **My hobby is . . .** , we say **I like . . . ing in my spare time**. We can also say **I like . . . ing in my free time** or **I'm interested in . . .**
Look at the following:

I like swimming **in my spare time.**
I really like skiing **in my free time.**
I'm interested in playing tennis.

So, instead of saying **What is your hobby**, you can ask **What do you like doing in your spare** (or **free**) **time**.

I'm crazy about it![2]   **It's okay.**[6]   **I can't stand it.**[8]
In daily conversation, there are many things we can say instead of **I like it** or **I don't like it**. Look at the following:

I like it.	I don't like it.	It's so-so.
I'm **crazy about** it.	I **can't stand** it.	It's **alright**.
I **love** it.	I **hate** it.	It's **okay**.
I think it's **great**.	It really **sucks**.	It's **reasonable**.

There aren't any swimmers.[3]

There aren't . . . or **there isn't . . .** means that something does not exist. Such *negative sentences* are easy to make. *Single objects* and *uncountable objects* use **there isn't** (or **there's not**): *Plural objects* use **there aren't**. Look at the following examples:

Single	Uncountable	Plural
There isn't a fast way to get rich.	**There isn't** any money in this money box.	**There aren't** any flies in China!

When the sentence is about a person, people or a country, we can often use **have** instead of **there isn't/aren't**. (*See Lesson 4 Language Notes again: page 37-39*)

Single	Uncountable	Plural
There isn't a bath in my house.	**There isn't** any love in his life.	**There aren't** any casinos in Japan.
I don't have a bath in my house.	He **doesn't have** any love in his life.	They **don't have** any casinos in Japan.

The meaning is the same.

There are 4 major strokes.[4]

There are . . . or **there is . . .** means that *something exists*. *Single* and *uncountable* objects use **there is** and *plural* objects use **there are**.

Single	Uncountable	Plural
There is a pretty girl over there!	**There is** some snow on the mountain.	**There are** many old buildings in Kyoto.

Sometimes we can use **have** instead of **there is/are**. (See examples above). **Have** *is not the same as* there is/are, there isn't/aren't, but the *meaning* is the same *sometimes*. This is usually when we talk about people or countries etc.

Single	Uncountable	Plural
There is a flea in your hair!	**There's** some money in my bag.	**There are** 3 foreigners in our company.
You have a flea in your hair!	**I have** some money in my bag.	**We have** 3 foreigners in our company.

The meaning is the same.

Aren't there any more?[5]

There is/are questions can be either positive or negative. The question is made by reversing the order of the two words. **There is** becomes **Is there**, **There are** becomes **Are there**, **There isn't** becomes **Isn't there** and **There aren't** becomes **Aren't there**. *Singular* and *uncountable* objects use **is/isn't**. *Plural* objects use **are/aren't**. Look at the following examples:

	IS	ARE
(+)	**Is there** a hotel near here?	**Are there** any questions?
(-)	**Isn't there** any toilet paper?	**Aren't there** any nice guys?

As in Language Notes 3 & 4, **have** can be used instead of **isn't/aren't there** in some cases. Look at the following:

Single (-)	Uncountable (+)	Plural (-)
Isn't there a library in this town.	**Is there** any salt on your table?	**Aren't there** any books in his desk?
Don't you **have** a library in this town?	**Do** you **have** any salt on your table?	**Doesn't** he **have** any books in his desk?

The meaning is the same.

It's too slow.[7]/ It's too difficult![9]

When we use the word **too** with adjectives or adverbs, **too** comes *before* the adjective or adverb. Look at the following:

He's **too** small.	Don't speak **too** fast.
You're **too** stupid.	You write **too** slowly!
That's **too** expensive.	She drives **too** dangerously.

There are always too many people.[10]/ It costs too much money.[11]

When we use the word **too** with nouns, we also have to use **many** with *countable* nouns, and **much** with *uncountable* nouns. These words come *before* the noun. Look at the following:

Uncountable	Countable
You have **too much** money.	He has **too many** girlfriends.
There is **too much** fighting in this world.	There are **too many** earthquakes in Japan.

We can also use **too** with verbs. In this case, we need to use the word **much** (not **many**). **Too much** comes *after* the verb. Look at the following:

> If you watch **too much** TV, you will get bad eyes.
> I think Takeshi drank **too much**.

There aren't enough pretty girls.[12]

The opposite of **too** or **too much** is **not enough**. **Not enough** means that the *number* or *amount* is *too small*. Look at the following examples.

Adjectives	O.J. was **not** smart **enough**. It's **not** hot **enough**, today.
Adverbs	He does **not** write neatly **enough**. They do **not** drive slowly **enough**.
Nouns	I have **not enough** money. There is **not enough** love in the world.
Verbs	You do **not** eat **enough**. We **never** practice **enough**.

(I do **not** have **enough** money is probably better here.)

5 - 5. Student Exercises: Fill in the blanks.
Choose the best sentence from the list below.

1	**Mr Fish:**	[ ]
2	**Mr Stone:**	Swimming pools. Yuck! [ ]
3	**Mr Fish:**	You don't like swimming? [ ]
4	**Mr Stone:**	Why do you like it? It's so boring! [ ]
5	**Mr Fish:**	[ ] It's a great sport.
6	**Mr Stone:**	[ ]
7	**Mr Fish:**	It's not expensive! It only costs three or four dollars.
8	**Mr Stone:**	[ ]
9	**Mr Fish:**	If you swim early in the morning, the pool is empty.
10	**Mr Stone:**	[ ]
11	**Mr Fish:**	If you practice, it's easy. Why don't you like swimming?
12	**Mr Stone:**	Because I can't swim!

Choose the best sentences for the blanks.
a) I can't stand swimming.
b) Swimming is too difficult!
c) Swimming doesn't suck!
d) Are there any swimming pools near your house?
e) It's too expensive.
f) I'm crazy about it!
g) It sucks!
h) There are always too many people in the pool.

5 - 6. Student Exercise: Select the best answer.

1.   Instead of saying **What is your hobby**, we can say
      (a)   What do you like doing   (b)   What do you like doing in
             in your spare time?   your hobby time?
      (c)   What do you like doing   (d)   All sentences are okay.
             in your play time?

2.   Which sentence means **I like watching horror movies**?
      (a)   Horror movies suck.   (b)   I can't stand horror movies.
      (c)   I'm crazy about horror   (d)   I think horror movies are
             movies.   reasonable.

3.   Instead of saying **They don't have any flies in China,** we can say:
      (a)   There aren't any flies in   (b)   There aren't no flies in
             China.   China.
      (c)   There isn't flies in China.(d)   There isn't no flies in China.

4.   Instead of saying **Isn't there a banana in your pocket**, we can say:
      (a)   Doesn't he have a banana(b)   Don't you have a banana in
             in his pocket?   your pocket?
      (c)   Do you have a banana in (d)   Do you not have bananas in
             your pocket?   your pocket?

5.   Which of the following sentences is NOT good?
      (a)   He is too heavy.   (b)   She has too much money.
      (c)   We run too slowly.   (d)   All sentences are okay.

6.   Which of the following sentences is NOT good?
      (a)   There are too many trees.(b)   She is too much crazy.
      (c)   You drive too quickly!   (d)   All sentences are okay.

7.   Which sentence is the opposite of **You eat too much**?
      (a)   You don't enough eat.   (b)   You don't eat enough.
      (c)   You eat not enough.   (d)   You don't eat not enough.

8.   Which sentence is the opposite of **There isn't enough water**?
      (a)   There is too many water. (b)   There are too many waters.
      (c)   There is too much water. (d)   There are too much water.

9.   Which word means **swimming method**?
      (a)   Strike.   (b)   Stroke.
      (c)   Stork.   (d)   Stuck.

10. Which of the following is NOT a style of swimming?
  (a) Freestyle.   (b) Dog-paddle.
  (c) Bodystroke.   (d) Butterfly.

5 - 7. Review of this lesson's major points. Do you understand these sentences and expressions?

I'm crazy about . . . ing	There isn't	too (adjective)
I love . . . ing	There aren't	too (adverb)
I think . . .ing is great	I don't have	too much (noun)
I can't stand . . . ing	There is	too many (noun)
I hate . . . ing	There are	not (adjective) enough
. . . ing sucks	I have	not (verb) (adverb) enough
. . . ing is allright	Is/are there	not enough (noun)
. . . ing is okay	Do you have	not (verb) enough
. . . ing is reasonable	Isn't/aren't there	I like . . . ing in my free time
(We can use **. . . ing**	Don't you have	I like . . ing in my spare time
or **a noun** or **it**.)		I'm interested in . . . ing.

5 - 8. Student exercise: Spot the difference.
Look at the illustration on page 44. There are 5 differences between the top and bottom illustrations. Please describe the differences in the space below. (Hint: You should begin *In the top picture, there is . . .* or *In the bottom picture, the swimmer has . . . .* etc.)

(i) _____

(ii) _____

(iii) _____

(iv) _____

(v) _____

5 - 9. Student exercise: How well did you understand the first dialogue? Answer the following questions with **true** (T) or **false** (F). Circle the correct answer.

1.   The swimmer's name is Mark.   (T) or (F)

2. The swimmer can't stand swimming. (T) or (F)

3. There are 3 major strokes. (T) or (F)

4. The swimmer's favourite stroke is breaststroke. (T) or (F)

5. Backstroke is too difficult. (T) or (F)

6. The swimmer likes butterfly. (T) or (F)

7. Dog-paddle is for learning. (T) or (F)

8. The pool often has too many people and is too expensive. (T) or (F)

9. Freestyle is also called *the Australian crawl*. (T) or (F)

10. Swimming fins were invented in 1878. (T) or (F)

NOTES:

Did you know that snowboarding is based on the *monoski*. The *monoski* is 30 or 40 years old, but snowboarding began in the 1980s. It is similar to skateboarding and surfing. Unlike skiing, snowboarding does not use poles. Hard ski-style boots or soft boots can be worn. It is now the largest growing winter sport in the world. Board lengths vary from about 1.3 to 2 metres, with the average length being about 1.5 metres. Unlike skiing, surfing or skateboarding, our feet are unable to move. Turning is done by moving your body weight.

6:
SNOWBOARDING

LESSON FOCUS: the words "IT/THAT/ONE"

6 - 1. Dialogue: Hobbyman meets a snowboarder.

1	**Hobbyman:**	Hi! <u>It's a nice day!</u>[1]
2	**Boarder:**	Yeah, it's great. Hey - I know you! You're Hobbyman. You came here to learn about hobbies, didn't you?
3	**Hobbyman:**	<u>That's right.</u>[2] Nice to meet you.
4	**Boarder:**	<u>It's good to meet you, too.</u>[3] By the way, my name's Burton Morrow. Please call me Burton. I'm a snow-boarder.
5	**Hobbyman:**	When did you first start snowboarding?
6	**Boarder:**	<u>I started it about 6 years ago.</u>[4]
7	**Hobbyman:**	And did you buy a snowboard then?
8	**Boarder:**	No. <u>I first bought one 5 years ago.</u>[5] <u>Before that,</u>[6] I rented one for a year.
9	**Hobbyman:**	How much was your board?
10	**Boarder:**	<u>It was about $300.</u>[7]
11	**Hobbyman:**	And your boots?
12	**Boarder:**	<u>They were only $90.</u>[8]
13	**Hobbyman:**	<u>That's cheap!</u>[9] Ah, how long is your board?
14	**Boarder:**	<u>This one is 1.6 metres.</u>[10] My old one was 1.5 metres long.
15	**Hobbyman:**	I see. Please tell me more about snowboarding.
16	**Boarder:**	Well, it's easier than skiing. It's also safer than skiing.
17	**Hobbyman:**	<u>That's good!</u>[11] Did you come snowboarding with your friends today?
18	**Boarder:**	Yeah. <u>That's my friend Simms,</u>[12] on the black board.
19	**Hobbyman:**	I see him. Well, thanks for your time Burton. I gotta' go now.
20	**Boarder:**	<u>That's okay.</u>[13] Catch ya' later, Hobbyman.
21	**Hobbyman:**	Okay. See ya'.

6 - 2. Short Dialogues: More **"it/that/one"** sentences.

A: How's the weather?
B: It's cold and cloudy.

    *   *   *

A: I'm pleased to meet you.
B: It's nice to meet you too.

    *   *   *

A: What do you think of raw fish?
B: Raw fish? Yuck! I can't stand it.
A: Really? I like it!

    *   *   *

A: Do you like lemons?
B: Mmm, I really love them.
A: I like 'em, too.

    *   *   *

A: Have you got a video camera?
B: Yeah. I've got one at home.

    *   *   *

A: Whose snowboards are those?
B: This one is mine. That one's hers.

    *   *   *

A: Do you prefer soccer or baseball?
B: They are both exciting!
A: I see. So, you like them both.

    *   *   *

A: Do you like big cars or small cars?
B: I like big ones.

    *   *   *

A: I won two million dollars!
B: Wow! That's wonderful!

    *   *   *

A: Thanks for helping me.
B: That's okay.

    *   *   *

A: Didn't you ski Mt Everest?
B: Yeah. That's right.
A: Wow! That's amazing!

    *   *   *

A: I only paid two hundred dollars for my snowboard.
B: That's cheap! You're lucky.

    *   *   *

A: I failed my driving test!
B: Oh dear! That's too bad.

    *   *   *

A: Who's the tall, bald guy?
B: Oh, that's Kojak.

    *   *   *

A: Would you like to come fishing with us tomorrow?
B: Thanks. That sounds like fun.

    *   *   *

A: Did you know James Dean was only 24 when he died?
B: Really? That's interesting!

    *   *   *

6 - 3. New Vocabulary: Do you know these words?

Board: **Board** means *snowboard*.
Boarder: **Boarder** means *snowboarder*.

6 - 4. Language Notes: Language Notes

It's a nice day!¹
We often use the word **it** when we are talking about the weather. Look at the
following examples:

How's the weather today? **It's** a nice day.
Look at those clouds! **It's** going to snow soon.
It was minus 15 degrees, yesterday!
Oh no! **It's** raining again.

That's right.² That's cheap!⁹ That's good!¹¹ That's okay.¹³
That is a very, very useful word. It is often followed by the "**be** verb" and an
adjective. These short sentences are very common and useful expressions in
daily converstaion. Look at the following very carefully:

THAT sentence	Meaning
That's right!	You are correct. What you say is true.
That's cheap! (Don't just say *Cheap*.)	The price, fee, cost or charge is cheap.
That's good! (Also *great, wonderful,* *excellent* etc)	Some news or information is favourable.
That's okay. That's alright. (In conversational English, *No problem* is also very common.)	You're welcome. Don't mention it. etc That is not a problem.
That's too bad! (Also *Too bad.*)	Some news or information is very sad or unfortunate. I'm sorry about that.
That's terrible! (Also *That's bad* and *That sucks.*)	Some news or information is bad.

In many of these cases, we can say **It's** instead of **That's**. The meaning is the same. However, in usual conversation, **it** *is not the same as* **that**. Look at the following examples: (*The meaning is the same here.*)

That's cheap. ◄► **It's** cheap. **That's** too bad. ◄► **It's** too bad.	**That's** great! ◄► **It's** great! **That's** okay. ◄► **It's** okay.

It's good to meet you, too.[3] (Review of Lesson 1 - *See page 8*)
When you meet somebody for the first time, after you have said your name, you can say (**It's**) **nice to meet you**. There are two types of greetings: There is the **It's** type and the **I'm** type. In both cases, **It's** and **I'm** can be omitted. Look at the following:

"It's" greetings	**"I'm" greetings**
(**It's**) nice to meet you. (**It's**) good to meet you. (**It's**) great to meet you.	(**I'm**) pleased to meet you. (**I'm**) glad to meet you. (**I'm**) happy to meet you.

I started it about 6 years ago.[4] **I first bought one 5 years ago.**[5]
Look at the following questions and answers.

When did you start *snowboarding*? Do you like *snow*? ➤ When did you buy your *car*?	I started **it** about 6 years ago. No, I don't like **it**. I bought **it** last week.
Did you buy *a* snowboard? Have you ever had *a* hangover? ➤ Would you like *a* coffee?	Yeah. I bought **one** yesterday. No. I've never had **one**. No thanks. I just had **one**.

Can you see the shortcuts?

> *snowboarding*, *drinking*, *car* ─────────────➤ **it**
> (*Singular* nouns, *uncountable* nouns and *verbs in the "-ing form"*)
> **a** snowboard, **a** hangover, **a** coffee ─────────➤ **one**
> (*Singular* nouns that take an *"a"*)

In the same way, plural nouns can be shortened to **them**. In conversation, the word **them** is sometimes shortened to **"'em"**. (Slang) See below:

Where did you buy your boots?	I bought **'em** (**them**) in Sydney.

Before that,[6]
That is also used with time. We often say **before that, . . .** or **after that, . . .**
After that is the same as *then*.

It was about $300.[7] They were only $90.[8]
It is often used with money. *Plural* nouns use **they**. Look at the following:

How much is this snowboard? →	**It's** $300.
And how much are the boots? →	**They** are only $90. ·

Of course, time also uses **It**. For example:

Excuse me. 'You got the time? →	Sure. **It's** 3 o'clock.

This one is 1.6 metres.[10]
One (meaning *a single item or person*) is often used with **this** and **that**. Look at the following examples:

Whose pens are these? →	**This one's** mine, and **that one's** his.
Do you like this car or that car?	I like **this one**.
Which boy hit you? →	**That one**!

We can also use the word **ones**. If we are talking about more than one object (*plural*), **this one** becomes **these ones** and **that one** becomes **those ones**. If we are talking about girls, **pretty ones** means *pretty girls*. If we are talking about cars, **fast ones** means *fast cars*. We use **ones** for *plural* objects. Look at the following :

Do you like red roses or pink roses? →	I like red **ones**.
John likes small dogs. →	Dolly like big **ones**.

That's my friend Simms.[12]
When introducing people, we often say *Mr A, **this** is Mr B*. If the person is NOT standing close to us, we often use **That**. For example:

Who's that guy over there?	**That's** my friend, Simms.
Who's the fat lady with the big nose?	**That's** my wife!

♪⑬🎥

6 - 5. Student Exercises: Fill in the blanks.
        Choose the best sentence from the list on the next page.

1 **Mr Simms:** Hey! Nice board! [   ]
2 **Mr O'Neil:** I got it in California. [   ]
3 **Mr Simms:** Wow. [   ] It's a new model, isn't it?
4 **Mr O'Neil:** [   ]It's very light and I like the colour.
5 **Mr Simms:** Yeah. What colour was your old board?

6   **Mr O'Neil:** [   ]
7   **Mr Simms:** Yeah, your old board.
8   **Mr O'Neil:** It was dark brown. Hey, who's the guy on the purple board?
9   **Mr Simms:** [   ] He's a friend of mine.
10   **Mr O'Neil:** I see. Are you snowboarding tomorrow?
11   **Mr Simms:** Yeah. [   ] Tomorrow will be a
         perfect day for snowboarding.
12   **Mr O'Neil:** [   ]

Choose the best sentences for the blanks.
a)   That's cheap!   e)   It was only $280.
b)   That's Nitro.   f)   That's great!
c)   It's going to snow tonight.   g)   That's right!
d)   My old one?   h)   Where did you buy it?

6 - 6. Student Exercise: Select the best answer.

1.   Instead of saying **You're welcome**, we can say:
     (a)   That's too bad.   (b)   That's amazing.
     (c)   That's good.   (d)   That's okay.

2.   If we hear some sad or unlucky news, we should say:
     (a)   That's great.   (b)   That's too bad.
     (c)   That's alright.   (d)   That's interesting.

3.   The question is **How's the weather?** The best answer is:
     (a)   It's fine.   (b)   That's fine.
     (c)   I'm fine.   (d)   Very nice, thanks.

4.   Which sentence is bad?
     (a)   It's nice to meet you.   (b)   It's great to meet you.
     (c)   It's good to meet you.   (d)   It's pleased to meet you.

5.   The question is **When did you start learning English?** The best
     answer is:
     (a)   I started one last year.   (b)   I started them last year.
     (c)   I started those last year. (d)   I started it last year.

6.   The question is **Would you like a beer?** The best answer is:
     (a)   No thanks. I just had it. (b)   No thanks. I just had ones.
     (c)   No thanks. I just had one.(d)   No thanks. I just had them.

7.   Instead of saying **then**, we can say:
     (a)   Before that,   (b)   After that,
     (c)   Then that,   (d)   That,

8. The question is **How much were your new skis?** The best answer is:
   (a) It was $400.
   (b) They was $400.
   (c) It were $400.
   (d) They were $400.

9. Rie and her mother are talking about sumo wrestlers. What does Rie say?
   (a) I like fat one.
   (b) I like fat ones.
   (c) I like fat.
   (d) I like fats.

10. Instead of saying **snowboarder**, we can say:
    (a) boarder.
    (b) skier.
    (c) snowboarding.
    (d) surfer.

6 - 7. Review of this lesson's major points. Do you understand these sentences and expressions?

It's cold.	That's great.	It's nice to meet you.
. . . it	That's too bad.	It's great to meet you.
. . . one	That's okay.	It's good to meet you.
. . . ones	That's alright.	It's 6pm.
. . . them	(No problem.)	Before that,
This one	That's cheap.	It is/was . . .
That one	That's terrible.	They was/were . . .
'em = them	That's = It's	That's my friend, John.
(*slang*)	(*sometimes*)	That sounds like fun.

6 - 8. Student Exercise: Complete the following Crossword. (Clues on next page.)

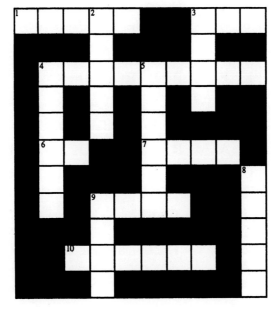

Across	**Down**
1) No problem = _ _ _ _ _ okay.	2) This one is mine. _ _ _ _ _ ones are yours.
3) I had a coffee but my wife didn't want _ _ _ .	3) That's alright = That's _ _ _ _ .
4) A **boarder** rides on a _ _ _ _ _ _ _ _ _ .	4) Snowboarding is safer than _ _ _ _ _ _ .
6) I cooked a steak, but my dog ate _ _ .	5) The opposite of **after that** is _ _ _ _ _ _ **that**.
7) Bill likes old cars, but James likes fast _ _ _ _ .	8) That's correct = That's _ _ _ _ _ .
9) Nice shoes. Where did you buy _ _ _ _ ?	9) My snowboard boots were cheap. _ _ _ _ were only $40.
10) Before buying a board, Burton Simms _ _ _ _ _ _ one.	

6 - 9. Student Exercise: Below is a list of snowboarding words. Can you find all of them in the word search below? Words are hidden horizontally - (left to right), vertically - (top to bottom) and diagonally - (top left to bottom right). Target time is **two minutes**.

```
N  I  T  R  O  S  K  I  I  N  G  S
S  N  G  B  O  A  R  D  E  R  S  T
I  S  N  O  W  B  O  A  R  D  G  H
M  S  P  E  E  D  G  S  B  J  T  A
M  T  O  H  A  I  R  W  A  L  K  R
S  P  E  E  O  P  L  E  N  K  S  D
O  N  E  I  L  B  B  O  A  V  O  B
K  E  M  P  E  R  B  U  R  J  F  O
P  O  W  D  E  R  T  Y  R  J  T  O
B  I  N  D  I  N  G  S  M  T  A  T
M  A  M  B  O  S  N  O  W  A  O  S
G  O  O  F  Y  L  S  S  J  T  N  N
```

Airwalk	Goofy	Nitro	Skiing
Bindings	Hard	Oneil	Snow
Boarder	Hobbyman	Plenk	Snowboard
Boots	Kemper	Powder	Soft
Burton	Mambo	Simms	Speed

6 - 10. Student exercise: How well did you understand the first dialogue?
         Answer the following questions with **true** (T) or **false** (F). Circle the
         correct answer.

1.   The boarder's name is Mr Burton Kemper.   (T) or (F)

2.   Burton is a skier.   (T) or (F)

3.   Burton started snowboarding 6 years ago.   (T) or (F)

4.   Burton's snowboard was $400.   (T) or (F)

5.   Burton's boots were $90.   (T) or (F)

6.   Burton's new board is 1.65 metres long.   (T) or (F)

7.   Burton's old board was 1.5 metres long.   (T) or (F)

8.   Snowboarding is more difficult than skiing.   (T) or (F)

9.   Burton's friend's name is Simms.   (T) or (F)

10.   Snowboarding began in the 1960s.   (T) or (F)

NOTES:

....

....

....

....

....

....

....

....

Did you know that martial arts means self defence. Nowadays, there are many martial arts, but all are based on techniques originating in Ancient China, India or Tibet. Japanese martial arts include *shorinji kempo*, *aikido*, *kendo*, *karate* and *judo*. China has martial arts such as *kung fu* and *wushu*, and Korea has *tae kwon do*. All of these martial arts are for self defence, but are usually practiced as sports. Hong Kong's *Bruce Lee* (dead) and *Jackie Chan* and America's *Jon van Damme* and *Steven Segal* are martial arts experts.

7: MARTIAL ARTS

LESSON FOCUS: the verb "GET"

♫⑭🎥

7 - 1. Dialogue: Hobbyman meets Bruce the martial arts expert.

1	**Hobbyman:**	Hi there! You're Bruce, aren't you. I saw you on TV.
2	**Bruce:**	Yeah. And you're hobbyman. I've heard about you. Nice to meet you.
3	**Hobbyman:**	Great to see you too, Bruce. Anyway, please tell me about your hobby.
4	**Bruce:**	Okay. I'm crazy about martial arts.
5	**Hobbyman:**	I see. How did you get into martial arts?[1]
6	**Bruce:**	Well, when I was a kid, I was really small. When I got to school,[2] the other kids always picked on me. They always said, "We're gonna' get you!"[3]
7	**Hobbyman:**	Oh - I get it![4] You started martial arts because kids picked on you!
8	**Bruce:**	Well, yes and no. I always got away,[5] but at that time, I got a really bad cold.[6] I couldn't get over it,[7] so I went to hospital. When I got out of hospital,[8] I wanted to get fit and healthy,[9] so I started martial arts.
9	**Hobbyman:**	Do you train hard?
10	**Bruce:**	Yeah. I get up at 6[10] and train for 2 hours. After work, I also train for 2 hours. I get home at 9.[11]
11	**Hobbyman:**	Well, thanks for talking to me, Bruce. It's getting late,[12] so I gotta' get outa' here.[13]
12	**Bruce:**	Okay Hobbyman. Before you go, I have a question.
13	**Hobbyman:**	Sure. What?
14	**Bruce:**	Where did you get that cape?[14]
15	**Hobbyman:**	I got it from my mother.[15]
16	**Bruce:**	I see. It's a nice colour.
17	**Hobbyman:**	Thanks, Bruce. Anyway, I gotta' go. See ya' later.
18	**Bruce:**	Okay. G'bye Hobbyman.

7 - 2. Short Dialogues: More "**get**" sentences.

A: How did you get into karate?
B: My Dad was a karate teacher.
A: I see.

    *   *   *

A: What time do you get to school?
B: I usually get to school at about 9.

    *   *   *

A: If you tell the police, we're gonna' get you!
B: Okay. I won't say anything.

    *   *   *

A: Did the police catch the robber?
B: No. He got away.

    *   *   *

A: Do you understand what I said?
B: No, I'm sorry. I don't get it.

    *   *   *

A: What's wrong with you. You look sick!
B: Yeah, I know. I've got the 'flu.!

    *   *   *

A: You look better now. Has your cold gone?
B: Yes, thanks. I got over it.

    *   *   *

A: I thought you were in hospital!
B: I was, but I got out on Friday.

    *   *   *

A: You are not allowed in this room. Get out!
B: I'm sorry.

    *   *   *

A: Chad, you are too heavy!
B: Yeah, I really have to get fit.

    *   *   *

A: Gee! It's already 9pm. It's getting late, so I have to go.
B: Okay. See ya' later.

    *   *   *

A: What time did you get up?
B: I got up at about 7.

    *   *   *

A: What time did you get home?
B: I can't remember.

    *   *   *

A: Oh no! It's already 2 am. I really gotta' get out of here.
B: Yeah, it's late, isn't it.

    *   *   *

A: Hey, nice shirt! Where did you get it?
B: It was a birthday present.

    *   *   *

A: When did you get married?
B: I got married 1 month ago.

    *   *   *

7 - 3. New Vocabulary: Do you know these words?

Martial- **Martial arts** means *self defence*. e.g. Shorinji Kempo, Aikido,
arts: Judo, Karate, etc.
Pick on: **Pick on** means *tease* or *harass*.
Robber: A **robber** is a person that steals thing; the same as a *thief*.
The 'flu: **The 'flu** means *influenza* or *a bad cold*.

7 - 4. Language Notes: Language Notes

How did you get into martial arts?[1]

Get into means *become involved in* or *become interested in*. It is very common in everyday conversation. Look at the following examples:

When did you **get into** painting, → When did you *become* Vincent?	*interested in* painting, Vincent?
Why did you **get into** making → Why did you *become interested* movies, Steven?	*in* making movies, Steven?

When I got to school, . . .[2] I get home at 9.[11]

Get sometimes means *arrive at* or *reach*. Look at the following:

My Dad and I leave home at 8. →	My Dad and I leave home at 8.
I **get to** school at 8:30. →	I *reach* school at 8:30.
He **gets to** work at 9. →	He *arrives* at work at 9.
I **get home** at about 3:30. →	I *arrive* at my house at 3:30.
He **gets back home** at 7pm. →	He *arrives back home* at 7pm.

"We're gonna' get you!"[3]

This expression is very slang. **"We're gonna' get you"** means *"We are going to get you"*. In this case, **. . . going to get . . .** means *tease*, *hurt* or *punish*. e.g.

If you tell the teacher, **we're** →	If you tell the teacher, *we're go-*
gonna' get ya'.	*ing to hit, hurt and punish you!*

Oh - I get it![4]

I get it means *I understand*. Also, *I follow you* and *I'm with you*. **I don't get it** means *I don't understand*. This is the same as *I don't follow you* or *I'm not with you*. The question forms are **Do you get it**, *Do you follow me* and *Are you with me*.

	Meaning	Get it	Others	
(+)	I understand.	I **get it**.	I follow you.	I'm with you.
(-)	I don't understand.	I don't **get it**.	I don't follow you.	I'm not with you.
(?)	Do you understand.	Do you **get it**.	Do you follow me.	Are you with me.

I always got away.[5]

Get away has 2 meanings in English conversation. One meaning is *escape*. The other meaning, used as a command, is *don't come here* or *don't go there*. Look at the following:

Escape	The 3 men chased me, but I **got away**.
Don't go there!	That bridge is dangerous. **Get away** from there!

I got a really bad cold.[6]

We can use **get** when we talk about health. In this case, **get** means *catch* or *have*. Look at the following examples:

> I **got** a really bad cold last week, but I'm okay now.
> If you **get** a tooth-ache, you should go to the dentist.

I couldn't get over it.[7]

Get over means *get well* or *recover from*. We use **get over** when we talk about *physical* or *emotional* problems. For example:

> Her father died 5 years ago. She still cannot **get over** his death.
> I had a very bad cold. It took 2 or 3 weeks to **get over** it.

When I got out of hospital, . . .[8] I gotta' get outa' here.[13]

Get out (of) means *leave*. **Get out** is very common in conversational English. Look at the following examples:

> I'm so happy! My mother got out of hospital yesterday, and my brother **gets out** of prison today.
> Oh no! It's midnight! I gotta' **get outa'** here. (*get outa' = get out of*)

Get fit and healthy.[9]

Get also means *become*. This is often used with adjectives. For example:

> John **got** old and weak. ➤ John *became* old and weak.
> I want to **get** well soon. ➤ I want to *become* well soon.

I get up at 6.[10]
Get up means *get out of bed*. This is different to **wake up**. **Wake up** means *finish sleeping*.

It's getting late . . . [12]
It's getting late means *it's becoming late*. This expression is used when somebody wants to leave a group of people or go back home. (*See Language Note 9 again.*) Look at the following example:

Wow! It's only 2am. Let's go to another bar!	⟶	It's **getting late**. I think I'd better go home.

Where did you get that cape?[14] **I got it from my mother.**[15]
Get can mean *acquire*, *buy* or *find*. Look at the following examples:

"Get" sentence	Meaning
Where did you **get** that cape?	Where did you *buy* that cape? or *How* did you *acquire* that cape?
I **got** it from my mother.	My mother *gave* it to me. or My mother *bought* it for me. or My mother *made* it for me.

This **get** is very common in everyday English conversation.

♪⑥🎥

7 - 5. Student Exercises: Fill in the blanks.
   Choose the best sentence from the list on the next page.

1	**Steven:**	Hey Jackie. [ ]
2	**Jackie:**	My Dad taught me. He's a kung fu teacher. How 'bout you?
3	**Steven:**	[ ] so I went to Japan and studied karate.
4	**Jackie:**	I see. Do you still train hard?
5	**Steven:**	Sure. [ ]
6	**Jackie:**	12 hours? [ ]
7	**Steven:**	Of course. [ ]
8	**Jackie:**	[ ] Why do you train so hard?
9	**Steven:**	If I don't train hard, I can't make any movies. If I don't make any movies, I can't get any money!
10	**Jackie:**	Okay. [ ]
11	**Steven:**	[ ] I'd better go. G'bye Jackie.
12	**Jackie:**	[ ] See ya' later Steve.

Choose the best sentences for the blanks.

a) Don't you get tired?
b) I don't get it, Steven.
c) I've gotta' get out of here, too.
d) When I get home, I go straight to bed.
e) How did you get into martial arts?
f) I get up at 6 and train for 12 hours.
g) Now I get it!
h) I wanted to get fit,
i) Anyway, it's getting late.

7 - 6. Student Exercise: Select the best answer.

1. Instead of saying **I became interested in karate last year,** we can say:
   (a) I got up karate last year . (b) I got into karate last year.
   (c) I got out karate last year. (d) I got over karate last year.

2. **I get to work at 8** means:
   (a) I leave work at 8.   (b) I arrive at work at 8.
   (c) I work from 8.   (d) I start work at 8.

3. **Do you get it?** means:
   (a) Do you understand?   (b) Do you follow me?
   (c) Are you with me?   (d) All answers are okay.

4. **They can't get away from prison** means:
   (a) They can't make it.   (b) They can't come.
   (c) They can't recover.   (d) They can't escape.

5. Instead of saying **I got the 'flu last week,** we can say:
   (a) I received the 'flu last   (b) I became interested in the 'flu
       week.   last week.
   (c) I had the 'flu last week.   (d) I arrived at the 'flu last week.

6. **She got over her bad cold** means:
   (a) She caught a bad cold.   (b) Her cold became very bad.
   (c) She never catches a cold. (d) She recovered from her cold.

7. Instead of saying **I have to get out of here,** we can say:
   (a) I must leave.   (b) I have to get home.
   (c) I have to get up now.   (d) I should get here soon.

8. **I want to become rich** is the same as:
   (a) I want to get over rich. (b) I want to get up rich.
   (c) I want to get rich.   (d) I want to get into rich.

9. If you are with a group of people, and you want to go home, you can say:
   (a) It's getting late. . .   (b) I'm getting late. . .
   (c) It got late . . .   (d) I'm late. . .

10.   Which martial arts expert is dead?
      (a)   Bruce Lee.   (b)   Steven Segal.
      (c)   Jackie Chan.   (d)   Jon van Damme.

7 - 7.   Review of this lesson's major points. Do you understand these sentences
         and expressions?

Martial arts	Get out of hospital	I get it.
Pick on	Get out of here	I follow you.
Robber	It's getting late.	I'm with you.
The 'flu	Get up	I don't get it.
Get into	Where did you get that?	I don't follow you.
Get to school	Get away	I'm not with you.
Get to work	Get a cold	Do you get it?
Get home	Get over it	Do you follow me?
Gonna' get you	Get fit	Are you with me?

7 - 8.   Student Exercise: Below is a list of martial arts words. Can you find all
         of them in the word search below? Words are hidden horizontally - (left
         to right), vertically - (top to bottom) and diagonally - (top left to bottom
         right). Target time is **two minutes**.

(Many Japanese martial arts words have become English - Look!)

```
D  C  H  O  P  H  O  L  D  K  F  D
E  K  E  N  D  O  K  Q  K  A  T  A
F  P  C  K  T  V  E  U  Z  E  N  Z
E  H  Q  S  H  O  R  I  N  J  I  F
N  S  B  L  O  C  K  R  J  G  V  K
C  K  F  A  I  K  I  D  O  W  F  W
E  A  T  A  E  K  W  O  N  D  O  U
U  R  B  E  L  T  D  O  J  O  Q  T
Q  A  P  U  N  C  H  T  L  O  J  H
Z  T  H  O  B  B  Y  M  A  N  N  R
G  E  X  J  U  D  O  K  I  C  K  O
J  U  J  I  T  S  U  T  U  F  T  W
```

Aikido	Dojo	Karate	Punch
Belt	Hobbyman	Kata	Shorinji
Block	Hold	Kendo	TaeKwonDo
Chop	Judo	Kick	Throw
Defence	Jujitsu	KungFu	Zen

7 - 9. Student Exercise: Can you see the hidden answer?

Chuck:	Which martial art technique is best, David?
David:	Well, there are so many . . .
Chuck:	That's right. I like *kicks*.
David:	Yeah, but *punches* and *chops* are very good.
Chuck:	And so are *throws*.
David:	Well . . . I suppose my favourite technique is (. . . . .).

To find out David's favourite martial art technique, please look at this stereogram carefully:

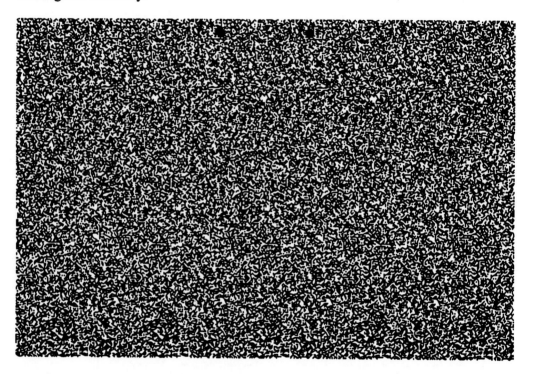

What is David's favourite technique? _____

7 - 10. Student exercise: How well did you understand the first dialogue?
Answer the following questions with **true** (T) or **false** (F). Circle the
correct answer.

1.   The martial arts expert's name is Jackie.   (T) or (F)

2.   Hobbyman saw him on TV.   (T) or (F)

3.   Bruce went to hospital when he was a kid.   (T) or (F)

4.   Bruce got into martial arts because his father was a karate teacher.   (T) or (F)

5.   Bruce gets up at 6 and trains for 3 hours.   (T) or (F)

6.   He gets home at 9 every night.   (T) or (F)

7.   After work, Bruce trains for 2 hours.   (T) or (F)

8.   When Bruce was a kid, the other kids picked on him.   (T) or (F)

9.   Hobbyman got his cape from his sister.   (T) or (F)

10.   Kung Fu is a Korean martial art.   (T) or (F)

NOTES:

DID YOU KNOW THAT ...

Did you know that the game of tennis first began around 1400. This form of tennis, first called *tenetz*, was played on an indoor court. There were high concrete walls, and the ball was allowed to bounce off them, like *squash*. Modern tennis was developed in 1873 in England. Tennis was introduced to America in 1874, and the first world championship was played at Wimbledon, in 1877. Since that time, the game's rules have not changed very much.

8: TENNIS

LESSON FOCUS: the verb "GIVE"

♫⑯📷

8 - 1. Dialogue: Hobbyman meets a tennis player.

1	**Hobbyman:**	Hi there! My name's Hobbyman. May I ask you some questions about your hobby?
2	**Boris:**	Sure. Ah, <u>give me a hand with this heavy bag.</u>[1]
3	**Hobbyman:**	Okay . . .(*Hobbyman helps Boris carry a heavy bag.*) . . . . . .umm, first, what's your name?
4	**Boris:**	My name's Boris.
5	**Hobbyman:**	Is that your <u>given name</u>[2]?
6	**Boris:**	Of course. My surname's Bicker.
7	**Hobbyman:**	And what do you like doing in your spare time, Boris?
8	**Boris:**	Don't you know? Take a look at my clothes! Look at my shoes! Look in my right hand!
9	**Hobbyman:**	Hmmm . . . I have no idea. <u>Give me a hint!</u>[3]
10	**Boris:**	Oh boy! My hobby is a ball sport. Here's the ball. Look at it! (*Boris gives the ball to Hobbyman.*[4])
11	**Hobbyman:**	I know! Are you a soccer player?
12	**Boris:**	Hobbyman! <u>Give me a break!</u>[5] Of course I'm not a soccer player!
13	**Hobbyman:**	Okay. <u>Give me more time.</u>[6] I've got it! Are you a golfer?
14	**Boris:**	Gee Hobbyman! <u>Are you kidding?</u>[7] <u>Why are you giving me such a hard time?</u>[8] I'm not a golfer!
15	**Hobbyman:**	Too difficult! <u>I give up!</u>[9] What's your hobby?
16	**Boris:**	I'm a tennis player, Hobbyman. This is a tennis racquet! <u>And please give me back my ball!</u>[10]
17	**Hobbyman:**	Okay, here you are! Gee, it's already 5 o'clock! I'd better go!
18	**Boris:**	Okay Hobbyman. If you want a game of tennis sometime, <u>give me a call.</u>[11]
19	**Hobbyman:**	Well, thankyou very much Boris, but <u>you didn't give me your phone number.</u>[12]
20	**Boris:**	Oh, really?

8 - 2. Short Dialogues: More "**give**" sentences.

A: This box is too big for me.
Could you <u>give</u> me a hand?

B: Sure. No problem.

     *   *   *

A: Is your surname Paul or Simon?

B: My <u>given name</u> is Paul and my
surname is Simon.

     *   *   *

A: What are you giving me for my
birthday? <u>Give</u> me a hint, please!

B: Okay. It's small but expensive. . .

     *   *   *

A: Wow! Nice car!

B: My father <u>gave</u> it to me.

A: Your father has too much money!

     *   *   *

A: Son, are you going to marry
her or not?

B: <u>Gimme'</u> a break, Dad. I haven't
decided, yet.

     *   *   *

A: Hurry up! We're late! Let's go!

B: I'm almost ready. Please <u>give</u>
me a bit more time!

     *   *   *

A: "Ladies and Gentlemen. I hope
you enjoyed the concert. Please
<u>give</u> the orchestra a hand."

B: (*Clap, clap, clap, clap* . . .)

     *   *   *

A: I'm getting married!

B: Are you <u>kidding</u>? You're
getting married? Amazing!

     *   *   *

A: You must study harder!!

B: Gee Dad! Why are you <u>giv-
ing</u> me such a hard time?

     *   *   *

A: What is the capital of Peru?

B: I have no idea. I <u>give</u> up!
Please tell me the answer.

     *   *   *

A: I lent you $10 last week.

B: I <u>gave</u> it back to your wife.

A: Oh no!

     *   *   *

A: If you want to speak to me,
<u>give</u> me a call.

B: What if you're not at home?

A: <u>Give</u> me a ring at work.

     *   *   *

A: I can't <u>give</u> you a call. You
didn't <u>give</u> me your number!

B: Oh! My number's 385-4411.

     *   *   *

A: Son. Marriage is <u>give</u> and
take.

B: I know! The man <u>gives</u> and
the woman takes!!

     *   *   *

8 - 3. New Vocabulary: Do you know these words?

Amazing: **Amazing** is the same as *Unbelievable* or *Incredible*. If we hear something which is very surprising, we can say these words.

Ball sport: A **ball sport** is *any sport which uses a ball*, such as *tennis*, *soccer*, *golf* or *rugby* etc.

Kidding: **Kidding** means *joking*. So **Are you kidding?** means *Are you joking?*

Oh boy! If we hear something surprising, exciting or disappointing, we can say **Oh boy**. There are many similar expressions, (often rude).

8 - 4. Language Notes: Language Notes

Give me a hand with this heavy bag.[1]
Give a hand has 2 meanings in conversational English. One meaning is *help*. The other meaning is *clap* or *applaud*. The first meaning is very common; the second is not so useful. Look at the following:

There is too much work. Could you **give me a hand**?	→	There's too much work. Could you *help* me?
I **gave** John **a hand** moving to his new apartment.	→	I *helped* John move to his new apartment.

Given name[2]
Saying *first name* or *last name* can sometimes be confusing. In several Asian countries, including Japan, the *last name* comes *first* and the *first name* comes *last*. For this reason, it is better to say **given name** instead of *first name* and **surname** instead of *last name* . Look at the following:

first name **given name** Christian name	last name **surname** family name

Give me a hint![3]
Hint uses the word **give**. If we want a hint, we *don't* say *Hint! Hint!* Look at the following example: (We can also say *clue* instead of **hint**.)

A:	What country do *Ferrari's* come from?
B:	*Ferrari's*? No idea! Please **give me a hint**.
A:	Okay. I'll **give you a hint**. The same country makes *Fiat* and *Alfa Romeo*.
A:	I got it! Italy!

Boris gives the ball to Hobbyman.[4]

This **give** is the basic **give**. The word order is interesting. Look at the following examples:

	person	give	thing	to	person
1	The policeman	**gave**	some candy	to	the little girl.
	Jack	**gave**	a bucket	to	Jill.
		Give	it	to	me!!

	person	give	person	thing
2	The policeman	**gave**	the little girl	some candy.
	Jack	**gave**	Jill	a bucket.
		~~Give~~	~~it~~	~~it~~

There are two ways of making the same sentence using **give**. It is okay to use **it** in the first type of sentence, (i.e. *person-give-thing-to-person*), but *not* in the second type of sentence, (i.e. *person-give-person-thing*). It *is* okay to use **that** in both types of sentences. e.g. **I gave that to him** & **I gave him that.**

Give me a break![5]

Give me a break is a very useful expression in conversational American English. The general meaning is *Don't tease me* or *Let me relax* or *Don't ask me any questions*. Look at the following example:

> **A:** Son, are you studying hard? Every year, your mother and I pay $10 000 to your university in fees. Are you the best student in your class? Do you always do your homework?
>
> **B:** Gee Dad! **Give me a break!** I'm doing my best!

Give me . . . is sometimes shortened to **gimme' . . .**, so people sometimes say **Gimme' a break**.

Give me more time.[6]

When we *need more time*, or *set time limits*, we often use the word **give**. Look at the following examples:

> - **Give** me 2 more days. I can't finish today.
> - I'm not ready yet. **Give** me 2 or 3 minutes, please.
> - I **gave** him a month, but he still hasn't paid back my money.
> - I'm **giving** you 5 seconds to answer my question!
> - I can't **give** you any more time. Give me your report now!

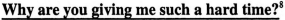

Are you kidding?[7]
Kidding means *joking*, so **Are you kidding** means *Are you joking*. This is a very common expression in everyday conversation. Another similar, good expression is *Are you serious*.

Why are you giving me such a hard time?[8]
Give a hard time means *tease* or *torment*. Expressions using **Give a hard time** are very common. It is similar to **Give me a break**. (*See Language Note 5*.)
Look at the following:

Don't **give** me such **a hard time**!	➤ Don't *tease* me!
Why did you **give** him such **a hard time**?	➤ Why did you *tease* him?
He always **gives** her **a hard time**.	➤ He always *teases* her.

I give up![9]
Give up is a very useful verb, and has many meanings.
One common meaning is *admit defeat* (*physical* or *mental*). So, if somebody says **Okay - I give up**, the meaning is *Okay - you win* or *I have no idea*. In this case, **give in** can also be used - the meaning is the same.
The second meaning is *stop* or *quit*. (**Give in** *can't* be used in this case.)
The third meaning is *lose hope*. (**Give in** also *cannot* be used in this case.)
Look at the following examples:

	give up	give in	meaning
1	**A:** What is H_2O? **B:** H_2O? I **give up**! Please tell me.	**A:** What is H_2O? **B:** H_2O? I **give in**! idea. Tell me.	In this case, **give up** means "I have no idea".
2	I **gave up** smoking 10 years ago.	~~I gave in smoking 10 years ago.~~	In this case, **give up** means "stop" or "quit".
3	My wife failed her driving test 18 times! I have **given up** on her!	~~My wife failed her driving test 18 times! I have given in on her!~~	In this case, **give up** means "lose hope".

And please give me back my ball![10]
Give back means *return something to it's owner*. For example, *John lent me $10 on Thursday. I gave it **back** to him on Friday*. (*See Language Note 4*).

Give me a call.[11]
Give me a call means *please call me by phone*. There are several verbs we can use. The following examples all have the same meaning.

Please **give** me **a call**.	Please *call* me.
Please *give* me *a ring*.	Please *ring* me.
Please *phone* me.	Please *telephone* me.

You didn't give me your phone number.[12]

Give me sometimes means *tell me*. Look at the following:

Give me your phone number.	*Tell* me your phone number.
She didn't **give** me her address.	She didn't *tell* me her address.
Please **give** me his name again.	Please *tell* me his name again.

♫📹🎥

8 - 5. Student Exercises: Fill in the blanks.
Choose the best sentence from the list on the next page.

1	**Steffi:**	Hey! Boris! [ ]
2	**Boris:**	I'm still using it. How about tomorrow?
3	**Steffi:**	[ ] I need it now!
4	**Boris:**	Oh Steffi! [ ]
5	**Steffi:**	Boris - you are a pain in the butt!*
6	**Boris:**	Thanks. [ ]
7	**Steffi:**	Your serve? What's the problem?
8	**Boris:**	I don't know. I always serve double faults.
		([ ])
9	**Steffi:**	This is my coach's number. [ ] He can help.
10	**Boris:**	[ ] I want you to help me.
11	**Steffi:**	[ ] Please call him. I don't want to help you.
12	**Boris:**	I'm not going to give back your tennis racquet!

*(**You are a pain in the butt** means *You are very annoying.*)

Choose the best sentences for the blanks.

a) Give me 2 more hours.
b) Steffi gives Boris a name card.
c) Give him a ring.
d) Um, could you give me a hand with my serve?
e) Give me back my tennis racquet!
f) Give me a break, Steffi.
g) Don't give me a hard time, Boris.
h) Boris, I gave my coach's number to you.

8 - 6. Student Exercise: Select the best answer.

1. **Given name** is the same as:
(a) Surname.
(b) First name.
(c) Family name.
(d) All answers are okay.

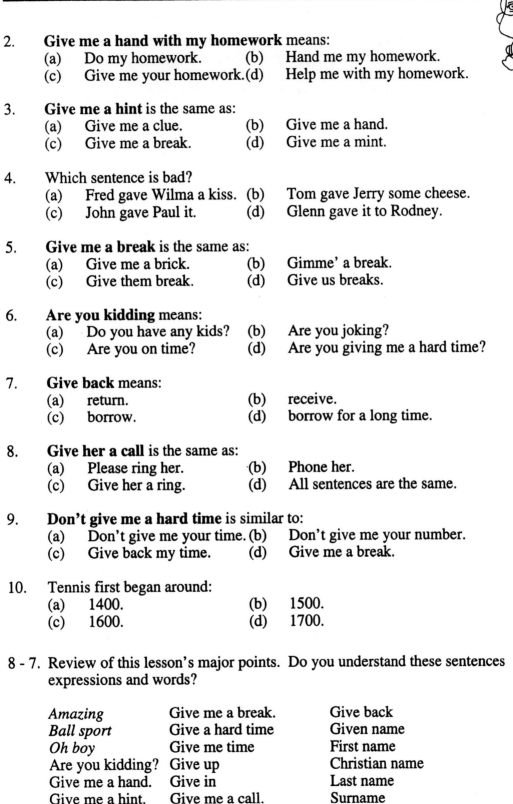

2. **Give me a hand with my homework** means:
   (a) Do my homework.   (b) Hand me my homework.
   (c) Give me your homework. (d) Help me with my homework.

3. **Give me a hint** is the same as:
   (a) Give me a clue.   (b) Give me a hand.
   (c) Give me a break.   (d) Give me a mint.

4. Which sentence is bad?
   (a) Fred gave Wilma a kiss. (b) Tom gave Jerry some cheese.
   (c) John gave Paul it.   (d) Glenn gave it to Rodney.

5. **Give me a break** is the same as:
   (a) Give me a brick.   (b) Gimme' a break.
   (c) Give them break.   (d) Give us breaks.

6. **Are you kidding** means:
   (a) Do you have any kids? (b) Are you joking?
   (c) Are you on time?   (d) Are you giving me a hard time?

7. **Give back** means:
   (a) return.   (b) receive.
   (c) borrow.   (d) borrow for a long time.

8. **Give her a call** is the same as:
   (a) Please ring her.   (b) Phone her.
   (c) Give her a ring.   (d) All sentences are the same.

9. **Don't give me a hard time** is similar to:
   (a) Don't give me your time. (b) Don't give me your number.
   (c) Give back my time.   (d) Give me a break.

10. Tennis first began around:
    (a) 1400.   (b) 1500.
    (c) 1600.   (d) 1700.

8 - 7. Review of this lesson's major points. Do you understand these sentences expressions and words?

Amazing	Give me a break.	Give back
Ball sport	Give a hard time	Given name
Oh boy	Give me time	First name
Are you kidding?	Give up	Christian name
Give me a hand.	Give in	Last name
Give me a hint.	Give me a call.	Surname
Give me a clue.	Give me your number.	Family name

8 - 8. Student Exercise: Below is a list of tennis words. Can you find all of them in the word search below? Words are hidden horizontally - (left to right), vertically - (top to bottom) and diagonally - (top left to bottom right). Target time is **three minutes**.

```
T  I  R  A  C  Q  U  E  T  W  X  K  C  T
A  R  Q  F  B  A  L  L  R  E  T  U  R  N
A  R  S  G  A  M  E  S  M  A  S  H  L  K
I  G  T  E  N  N  I  S  V  O  L  L  E  Y
F  L  A  T  T  Z  O  S  N  E  T  R  J  D
I  N  D  O  O  R  T  I  E  B  R  E  A  K
G  R  A  S  S  L  T  O  P  S  P  I  N
O  U  A  D  V  A  N  T  A  G  E  L  E  T
I  L  H  A  R  D  C  O  U  R  T  H  F  F
H  O  B  B  Y  M  A  N  D  E  U  C  E  A
Z  V  U  Q  Z  Z  A  H  J  L  A  W  N  U
D  E  R  T  N  G  H  T  S  E  R  V  E  L
D  R  I  V  E  J  R  E  C  E  I  V  E  T
W  I  M  B  L  E  D  O  N  H  D  U  J  L
```

Advantage	Grass	Match	Set
Ball	Hardcourt	Net	Smash
Deuce	Hobbyman	Out	Tennis
Drive	Indoor	Racquet	Tiebreak
Fault	Lawn	Receive	Topspin
Flat	Let	Return	Volley
Game	Love	Serve	Wimbledon

8 - 9. Student Exercise: STEREOGRAM. Can you see the hidden answer?

Björn: Isn't tennis a great game, Jimmy?
Jimmy: Yeah, it sure is! Actually, Björn, I have a question for you?
Björn: Sure. What is it?
Jimmy: Well, you won five tournaments at Wimbledon, didn't you?
Björn: Yes, that's right.
Jimmy: Well . . . how old were you when you won your first title?
Björn: Oh . . . I was (. . . . .) years old.

To find out how old Björn was when he first won Wimbledon, look at the stereogram on the next page very carefully.

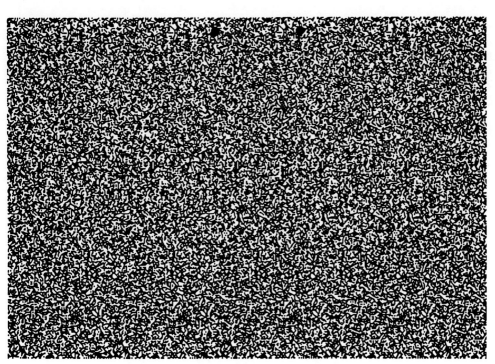

How old was Björn Borg when he first won Wimbledon? _____

8 - 10. Student exercise: How well did you understand the first dialogue? Answer the following questions with **true** (T) or **false** (F). Circle the correct answer.

1. The tennis player's surname is Boris. (T) or (F)

2. The tennis player has a heavy bag. (T) or (F)

3. Boris does not give a tennis ball to Hobbyman. (T) or (F)

4. Boris is holding a tennis racquet in his left hand. (T) or (F)

5. Tennis is not a ball sport. (T) or (F)

6. Boris is not wearing tennis clothes. (T) or (F)

7. Hobbyman thinks Boris is a golfer. (T) or (F)

8. Hobbyman leaves at five thirty. (T) or (F)

9. Boris tells Hobbyman his phone number. (T) or (F)

10. Modern tennis was developed in 1874 in England. (T) or (F)

DID YOU KNOW THAT ...

Did you know that an Englishman called *Charles Babbage* designed the first computer. Mr Babbage died in 1871, at the age of 79. The first electronic computer was built in America in 1946. Nowadays, there are many computer companies in the world. The first Apple computer (*now called Macintosh*) was built in a garage in 1976 by two young men. Computers have since become smaller, faster and cheaper and many people now have home computers and video games. (*This text was written on a computer.*)

9: COMPUTING

LESSON FOCUS: the verbs "TALK/ SAY/ SPEAK/ TELL"

♪⑱🎥

9 - 1. Dialogue: Hobbyman meets a computer hacker.

1	**Hobbyman:**	Hello! Is anybody there?
2	**Computer:**	Are you talking to me?[1]
3	**Hobbyman:**	Who's speaking?[2] I can't see anybody!
4	**Computer:**	I'm speaking.
5	**Hobbyman:**	Who said that?[3] Please tell me your name![4]
6	**Computer:**	My name's Mac.
7	**Hobbyman:**	Okay Mac, I can hear you, but I can't see you. Where are you?
8	**Computer:**	I'm in front of you! I'm Mac, the computer!
		(*Computer hacker comes in.*)
9	**Hacker:**	Hi there! How do you like my computer? The voice is good isn't it? You can't tell it's a computer.[5]
10	**Hobbyman:**	Who are you?
11	**Hacker:**	I'm Charles Cabbage. You were talking to my computer.
12	**Hobbyman:**	Ohh!! I get it . . . Your hobby is computing, right? Please tell me about it.[6]
13	**Hacker:**	Well, when I was a kid, my father always talked about computers.[7] He told me they were very important. Nowadays, they say most jobs use computers.[8]
14	**Hobbyman:**	Would you say computers will take peoples' jobs?[9]
15	**Hacker:**	No, I don't think so. Shall we talk it over with Mac?[10]
16	**Hobbyman:**	Okay. Let's ask Mac.[11]
17	**Hacker:**	Well, what do you think, Mac?
18	**Computer:**	Let me see. Generally speaking, computers are user-friendly.[12] Computers help people. We don't take jobs. We save time.
19	**Hobbyman:**	Speaking of time,[13] it's already 6. I have to go. Thanks for telling me about your hobby, Charlie. See ya' Mac.
20	**Computer:**	See you later, Hobbyman.
21	**Hacker:**	G'bye Hobbyman.

9 - 2. Short Dialogues: More "**say/speak/talk/tell**" sentences.

A: Excuse me. May I <u>talk</u> to you for a few minutes?
B: What do you want to <u>talk</u> about?

*   *   *

A: Please turn the music down!
B: What did you <u>say</u>?
A: I <u>said</u>, "Turn the music down."

*   *   *

A: Can you <u>speak</u> Japanese?
B: No, but I can <u>speak</u> French.

*   *   *

A: Please <u>tell</u> me your name, age and address.
B: No way! I'm not <u>telling</u> you anything!

*   *   *

A: Look at that long haired hippy!! Is it a boy or a girl?
B: I <u>can't tell</u>!

*   *   *

A: Please <u>tell</u> me <u>about</u> Australia.
B: Australia? Well, it's very, very big and very, very hot.

*   *   *

A: I went to see the Pope last week.
B: What did he <u>talk about</u>?
A: He <u>spoke about</u> peace, love and happiness.

*   *   *

A: It rained all day today!
B: <u>They say</u> that it's going to rain all day tomorrow, too.

*   *   *

A: <u>Would you say</u> she's pretty?
B: Yeah, I think so. <u>I'd say</u> she was really pretty.

*   *   *

A: May I <u>ask</u> you a question?
B: What would you like to <u>ask</u>?

*   *   *

A: Mum, can I go camping with my friends?
B: Well . . . let's <u>talk it over</u> with your father.

*   *   *

A: Do Japanese always eat rice?
B: <u>Generally speaking</u>, most Japanese eat rice every day.

*   *   *

A: I <u>spoke</u> to Johnny yesterday.
B: Really? <u>Speaking of</u> Johnny, where does he live now?

*   *   *

A: Please <u>tell</u> me what he <u>said</u>.
B: What <u>did</u> you <u>say</u>?
A: I <u>said</u>, "Please <u>tell</u> me what he <u>said</u>".

*   *   *

9 - 3. New Vocabulary: Do you know these words?

Hacker: A **hacker** or a **computer-hacker** is *an expert computer user or programmer*.

The Pope: **The Pope** is *the leader of the Roman Catholic branch of Christianity*. The current Pope is *Pope John Paul the Second*.

User-friendly: **User-friendly** means *easy to use* or *easy to learn to use*. This is a computer expression.

9 - 4. Language Notes: Language Notes

Are you talking to me?[1] Who's speaking?[2]
Talking and **speaking** are similar. Both words use either **to** or **with** to show the object. Look at the following examples:

talk to	talk with	speak to	speak with
I **talked to** him. They won't **talk to** us.	I **talked with** him. They won't **talk with** us.	I **spoke to** him. They won't **speak to** us.	I **spoke with** him. They won't **speak with** us.

What's the difference? These two verbs are very similar. **Speak** is *probably* better. Look at the following examples:

Can you **talk** Japanese?	Can you **speak** Japanese?
(on the telephone)	*(on the telephone)*
Hello, can I **talk** to John please?	Hello, can I **speak** to John, please?

   not so good okay   very good very good

In both examples, the **speak** sentences are the best. The **talk** sentences are okay, but **speak** is better.

Who said that?[3]
Say or **said** is used with people's spoken words. Look at the following:

A:	I'm busy!	A:	What did he **say**?
B:	What did you **say**?	B:	He **said**, "You are stupid!"
A:	I **said**, "I'm busy!"	A:	Oh. . . I see . . . Thank you.

Say is also used with *direct* and *indirect* sentences. Look at the following:

	Direct		**Indirect**
A:	What did she **say**?	A:	What did she **say**?
B:	She **said**, "I love you!"	B:	She **said** (that) she loved me.

*This is an example of a usual sentence in **direct** and **indirect** form.*

	Direct			Indirect
A:	What did they **say**?	→	A:	What did they **say**?
B:	They **said**, "Where do you live?"		B:	They **asked** me where I **lived**.

	Direct			Indirect
A:	What did they **say**?	→	A:	What did they **say**?
B:	They **said**, "Do you like *ume boshi*?"		B:	They **asked** me if I liked *ume boshi*.

*These are examples of questions in **direct** and **indirect** form.*

	Direct			Indirect
A:	What did you **say**?	→	A:	What did you **say**?
B:	I **said**, "Shut up!"		B:	I **told** you to shut up. (*Or* I **said** to shut up.)

	Direct			Indirect
A:	What did you **say**?	→	A:	What did they **say**?
B:	I **said**, "Don't speak to me!"		B:	I **told** you not to speak to me. (*Or* I **said** not to speak to me.)

*These are examples of commands in **direct** and **indirect** form.*

Indirect sentences are better than **direct** sentences in conversation. Using **direct** sentences sometimes causes confusion. Look at this simple summary:

Sentences:		**A said**	**(that)**	**S**	**V(past)**	**O**
	(I)	John said	(that)	he	was buying	a new car
	(D)	John said		"I	am buying	a new car."
Questions(1):		**A asked B**	**W?**	**S**	**V(past)**	**O**
	(I)	John asked me	when	I	was going	to Tokyo.
	(D)	John said	"When	are you	going	to Tokyo?"
Questions(2):		**A asked B**	**IF**	**S**	**V(past)**	**O**
	(I)	John asked me	if	I	liked	cabbage.
	(D)	John said	"Do	you	like	cabbage?"
Commands(1):		**A told B**	**TO**		**V(present)**	**O**
	(I)	John told me	to		go	home.
	(D)	John said			"Go	home"
Commands(2):		**A told B**	**NOT TO**		**V(present)**	**O**
	(I)	John told me	not to		watch	TV.
	(D)	John said	"Don't		watch	TV!"

Please tell me your name!⁴
Tell is often used for *information*. For example, we say:

Please **tell** me your name.	He **told** me his address.
Tell me where you met her.	Don't **tell** him your phone number.

You can't tell (that) it's a computer.⁵
Can't tell (that) means *we can't know the truth about something by looking or listening*. Look at the following examples:

A:	These two pens look the same? Which one's mine?	**A:**	Who did you speak to this morning, on the phone? Was it Anna or Hannah?
B:	Gee . . . **I can't tell!** Don't you know?	**B:**	I don't know. They sound the same! **I couldn't tell.**
A:	No. **I can't tell either!**		

Please tell me about it.⁶
Tell *someone* **about** is similar to **tell**, (*See language Note 4*) but the topic of conversation is wider. Look at the following examples:

1	**A:** **Tell me** your name. **B:** My name is Simon.	**A:** **Tell me about** your name. **B:** Well, Simon is an old English name. It means 'honest'.	

2	I'll **tell** you **about** Australia. Australia is 22 times larger than Japan, but only 18 million people live there.

When I was a kid, my father always talked about computers.⁷
Talk about means *discuss*. **Let's talk about soccer** means *Let's discuss soccer*. **Talk about** and *discuss* are both widely used.

They say (that) most jobs use computers.⁸
They say (that) . . . is the same as *It is said* . . . . This means that something is widely believed, or that most people think it is true. For example:

They say winter will be cold, this year.
They say Michael Jackson had lots of plastic surgery.
They say that people who drink beer rarely catch colds.

Would you say computers will take peoples' jobs?⁹
Would you say (that) . . . means *Do you think* . . . . The answer is **I'd say (that)** . . ., which means *I think* . . . . Look at the following:

A:	Would you say that Madonna is beautiful?	A:	*Do you think that* Madonna is beautiful?
B:	No. **I'd say** she's ugly.	B:	No. *I think* she's ugly.

Shall we talk it over with Mac?[10]
Talk . . . over means *discuss*. **Talk . . . over** is a little different to *talk about*, (*See Language Note 7*). **Talk . . . over** is used for discussing *problems* or *serious things*. **Talk about** is used for general discussion.

Let's ask Mac.[11]
Ask is the question verb. (**See Language Note 3**).

Generally speaking, computers are user-friendly.[12]
Generally speaking, . . . means *in most cases* or *usually*. For example, **Generally speaking, Japanese people have black hair.**

Speaking of time . . . [13]
Speaking of . . . is a very useful expression. We use **speaking of . . .** to *change the conversation topic.* Look at the following examples:

A:	Jimmy bought a new car.	A:	Jimmy bought a new car.
B:	**Speaking of cars**, have you seen the new model Jeep?	B:	**Speaking of Jimmy**, does he still work for IBM?

♫◉🎥

9 - 5. Student Exercises: Fill in the blanks.
Choose the best sentence from the list below and on the next page.

1	**Mr Jobbs:**	Hey! Aren't you Bill Gates?
2	**Mr Gates:**	[?]
3	**Mr Jobbs:**	Yes, I am. [ ]
4	**Mr Gates:**	That's right. I am the richest man in the world.
5	**Mr Jobbs:**	Wow! [ ]
6	**Mr Gates:**	[ ] I'm busy. Go away!
7	**Mr Jobbs:**	Oh, Mr Gates! Please tell me how I can get rich, too.
8	**Mr Gates:**	[ ]
9	**Mr Jobbs:**	I see. [?]
10	**Mr Gates:**	Yeah. [ ] It's easy - work hard, make money!
11	**Mr Jobbs:**	[ ]
12	**Mr Gates:**	No way! I'm rich, but I'm not stupid.

Choose the best sentences for the blanks.

a) I'd say you can.   e) Please tell me how you got so rich.
b) Are you talking to me?   f) Speaking of money, please lend me $10.

c)   Would you say I can get rich,   g)   I don't want to talk about it
      if I work hard like you?   with you!
d)   Generally speaking, if you   h)   They say you are the world's
      work hard, you can get rich.   richest man.

9 - 6.   Student Exercise: Select the best answer.

1.   **He talked to me** is similar to:
      (a)   He said to me.   (b)   He spoke to me.
      (c)   He asked to me.   (d)   He told to me.

2.   He said,"I'm eating." The *indirect* sentence is:
      (a)   He said he was eating.   (b)   He said I am eating.
      (c)   He said I was eating.   (d)   He said he ate.

3.   She said,"Kiss me!" The *indirect* sentence is:
      (a)   She said kiss me.   (b)   She said to kiss me.
      (c)   She said kiss her.   (d)   She said to kiss her.

4.   If 2 pens look the same and a friend says **Which is mine?**, you say:
      (a)   I wouldn't say.   (b)   I can't talk it over.
      (c)   I can't tell.   (d)   I can't speak about it.

5.   **Talk about** is the same as:
      (a)   Tell about.   (b)   Discuss.
      (c)   Ask about.   (d)   Say.

6.   **They say . . .** is the same as:
      (a)   They speak.   (b)   I say.
      (c)   It is said.   (d)   Speaking of.

7.   Which sentence is the best?
      (a)   Say me your address.   (b)   Speak me your address.
      (c)   Talk me your address.   (d)   Tell me your address.

8.   **Would you say . . .** means:
      (a)   Can you speak?   (b)   Do you think . . .
      (c)   Are you telling . . .   (d)   Are you saying . . .

9.   **Generally speaking, . . .** means:
      (a)   In most cases, . . .   (b)   I'm sure that . . .
      (c)   Saying honestly, . . .   (d)   Speaking of generals, . . .

10.   **Discuss *something* seriously** is the same as:
      (a)   Say about.   (b)   Tell about.
      (c)   Talk over.   (d)   Ask over.

9 - 7. Review of this lesson's major points. Do you understand these sentences expressions and words?

Hacker	Speak about	Talk to	They say
User-friendly	Talk about	Talk with	It is said
Say	Talk it over	Speak to	Would you say
Tell	Speaking of	Speak with	I'd say
Tell about	Generally speaking	Ask	Can't tell

9 - 8. Student Exercise: Below is a list of computer words. Can you find all of them in the word search below? Words are hidden horizontally - (left to right), vertically - (top to bottom) and diagonally - (top left to bottom right). Target time is **two minutes**.

```
M  U  L  T  I  M  E  D  I  A  E  H
D  R  I  V  E  H  Q  A  F  U  C  Z
B  J  A  Q  O  D  E  S  K  T  O  P
J  R  W  K  E  Y  B  O  A  R  D  P
F  H  D  A  C  O  M  P  U  T  E  R
I  A  I  J  P  R  I  N  T  E  R  O
L  R  S  E  R  V  E  R  N  K  R  C
E  D  P  B  I  T  B  Y  T  E  A  E
V  R  L  U  V  D  I  S  C  S  M  S
V  O  A  M  E  M  O  R  Y  A  R  S
I  M  Y  F  L  O  P  P  Y  V  K  O
M  O  U  S  E  Q  N  F  W  E  O  R
```

Bit	Display	Keyboard	Processor
Byte	Drive	Memory	Ram
Computer	File	Mouse	Rom
Desktop	Floppy	Multimedia	Save
Disc	Hard	Printer	Server

9 - 9. Student Exercise: STEREOGRAM. Can you see the hidden answer?

Mr Maeda: Would you say PC's are the best computers?
Steve: No way. They suck!
Mr Maeda: Well, what computers do you think are good?
Steve: Well . . . they say that the(. . . . .) is the best!

To find out the best computer, please look at this stereogram carefully:

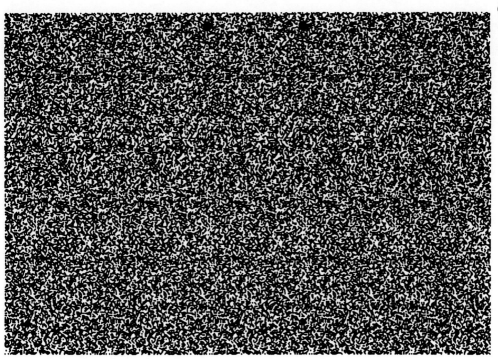

What is the best computer? _____

9 - 10. Student exercise: How well did you understand the first dialogue?
         Answer the following questions with **true** (T) or **false** (F). Circle the
         correct answer.

1.   The computer hacker's name is Charles Savage.   (T) or (F)

2.   The computer's name is Mac.   (T) or (F)

3.   Mac is behind Hobbyman.   (T) or (F)

4.   Charles's father never talked about computers.   (T) or (F)

5.   Computers are not usually user-friendly.   (T) or (F)

6.   Charles's father said computers were important.   (T) or (F)

7.   Mac thinks computers don't help people.   (T) or (F)

8.   Mac thinks computers save time.   (T) or (F)

9.   Hobbyman leaves at 6 o'clock.   (T) or (F)

10.   The first computer was designed over 100 years ago. (T) or (F)

DID YOU KNOW THAT . . .

Did you know that *Rollerblades*™ were invented in 1980 by a 20 year old Canadian ice hockey player, Scott Olsen, and his 16 year old brother, Brennan. They bought the patent from a company in Chicago, and perfected the design. They used a ski boot and a polyurethane blade and wheels. Now they are very rich, and rollerblades have become very popular all over the world.

10: ROLLERBLADES

LESSON FOCUS: the verbs "SEE/ WATCH/ LOOK"

♫ ⑳ 🎥

10 - 1. Dialogue: Hobbyman meets an in-line skater.

1	**Hobbyman:**	Hi there! That looks dangerous![1]
2	**Skater:**	Yeah, it is! These are called *rollerblades*™.
3	**Hobbyman:**	I can't see them very well.[2]
4	**Skater:**	Here, take a closer look.[3]
5	**Hobbyman:**	Thanks. Gee, they look like ice-skates.[4]
6	**Skater:**	Yes, they do, don't they?
7	**Hobbyman:**	Are they expensive?
8	**Skater:**	Well . . . let me see[5] . . . I paid $120, so they're not cheap.
9	**Hobbyman:**	I see.[6] Is roller-blading easy?
10	**Skater:**	I'm just learning, but I can skate a bit. Watch this![7]
11	**Hobbyman:**	Be careful! Oh no! Look out![8]
		(*Roller-blader hits a big tree.*)
12	**Skater:**	Ouch!
13	**Hobbyman:**	Are you okay? I told you to watch out.[9] Didn't you see that tree? You should look where you're going![10]
14	**Skater:**	I couldn't stop. Where are my glasses? I can't see my glasses!
15	**Hobbyman:**	Let's look for them.[11] Oh, here they are!
16	**Skater:**	Thanks!
17	**Hobbyman:**	I think you should see a doctor.[12] Your leg looks bad!
18	**Skater:**	Don't worry! My mother will look after me.[13]
19	**Hobbyman:**	Okay - anyway, thanks for your interesting rollerblade demonstration.
20	**Skater:**	I'll practice more, next time.
21	**Hobbyman:**	You do that. Anyway, I'll see you later.[14] Goodbye.
22	**Skater:**	'Bye.

10 - 2. Short Dialogues: More **"look/see/watch"** sentences.

A: Your shirt <u>looks</u> very nice!
B: Really? Thank you very much.

    *   *   *

A: Your car stereo <u>sounds</u> good.
B: Thanks. It's new. It really <u>sounds</u> great, doesn't it.

    *   *   *

A: Hey. <u>Take a look</u> at that car!
B: Wow! A Ferrari! Very nice!

    *   *   *

A: Can you <u>see</u> the sea from here?
B: On a good day, we can <u>see</u> it.

    *   *   *

A: Don't you think she <u>looks like</u> Marilyn Monroe?
B: No, I don't. I think she <u>looks like</u> Hulk Hogan.

    *   *   *

A: What's your girlfriend's name?
B: <u>Let me see</u> . . .I can't remember!

    *   *   *

A: Why did you leave so early?
B: I was feeling sick.
A: Oh, <u>I see</u>.

    *   *   *

A: Did you <u>watch</u> the news last night?
B: No, I <u>watched</u> the wrestling.

    *   *   *

A: Oh my God! <u>Look out!</u>
B: Ahhhhhhh! Ouch!

    *   *   *

A: Didn't you <u>see</u> that car? I told you to <u>watch out</u>!
B: Sorry. I wasn't concentrating·

    *   *   *

A: What are you <u>looking at</u>?
B: Those pretty girls over there.

    *   *   *

A: What are you <u>looking for</u>?
B: I dropped my contact lens.

    *   *   *

A: Ow! My leg really hurts!
B: Why? What did you do?
A: I hit a tree while I was skiing.
B: You should <u>see</u> a doctor!

    *   *   *

A: Where is your son?
B: My wife is <u>looking after</u> him.

    *   *   *

A: Well, it's getting late, so I'd better go now. <u>See ya'</u>.
B: Okay. I'll <u>see you</u> later.

    *   *   *

A: Did you <u>see</u> John today?
B: No. I'll meet him tomorrow.

    *   *   *

10 - 3. New Vocabulary: Do you know these words?

Inline skates: **Inline skates** refer to any skates where the wheels are in a row, or "in-a-line".

Rollerblades: **Rollerblades**™ is the registered trademark name of the original brand of inline skates. Many people say **Rollerblades** or **'blades** when referring to inline skates.

Rollerblader: A **Rollerblader** is an inline skater.

10 - 4. Language Notes: Language Notes

That looks dangerous![1]
Looks is often used with adjectives. **That looks dangerous** means *That seems* (or *appears*) *dangerous*. We can use other *sense words* in the same way.

	Subject	Sense	Adjective
Look →	That house	**looks**	really old.
Taste →	This steak	tastes	very good.
Sound →	That band	sounds	terrible!
Smell →	Your cooking	smells	wonderful.
Feel →	Your hair	feels	so soft.

I can't see them very well.[2]
See is the basic *eye-verb*. It means *notice with the eye*. **See** is often used with *can*. Other words, such as **look** or **watch** rarely use *can*.

I **saw** the fireworks display yesterday.	I can't **see** my mother.
We can **see** Mt Fuji from our house.	I've never **seen** him before.

Take a closer look.[3] You should look where you're going![10]
Look means *pay attention to a particular object*. **Take a look** or **have a look** has the same meaning, but the time is perhaps *a little shorter*.

Look →	**Look** at that big horse! Don't **look** at the sun.
Take a look	**Take a look** at this plant. I **had a** quick **look** at his house.

They look like ice-skates.[4]
Look like is used with nouns. **Look** *must not be used alone* with nouns. **He looks like a pro-wrestler** means *He seems* (or *appears*) *to be a pro-wrestler*. We can also use other *sense words* (with *like*), in the same way. Look at the following examples:

	Subject	Sense	Noun
Look like →	That girl	**looks like**	Marilyn.
Taste like →	This coffee	tastes like	mud.
Sound like →	That car	sounds like	a toy.
Smell like →	Your breath	smells like	a brewery.
Feel like →	This jacket	feels like	leather.

Let me see . . . [5]

Let me see . . . is used while we are thinking, or not sure what to say. It is the same as *Ah . . .* , *Um . . .* , *Well . . .* and *Er . . . .*

I see. [6]

I see means *I understand.* If somebody explains something to you, you can say **I see what you mean.**

Watch this! [7]

Watch means *look carefully for a length of time, usually for a purpose.* We often use the word **watch** with *TV*, *shows*, *games*, *presentations* etc.

> John's **watching** TV and Sue-Ellen's watching the football game.
> If you go to a magic show, **watch** the magician carefully!

Look out! [8] I told you to watch out. [9]

Look out and **watch out** are warnings. They mean *Be careful* or *Danger.*

Let's look for them. [11]

Look for is the same as *search (for)* or *hunt.* Look at the following:

> I've lost my car keys. Please help me **look for** them.
> Glenn's **looking for** a nice girl to marry, but he can't find one.

I think you should see a doctor. [12]

See sometimes means *visit* or *meet.* We often use **see** when we make an appointment with someone. We also use **see** when we visit or meet friends.

Appointment	I have to **see** the doctor tomorrow. I'd like to **see** the manager, please.
Meet / Visit	I **saw** Frank yesterday. He didn't look well. I haven't **seen** your husband recently. How is he?

My mother will look after me.[13]
Look after means *care for* or *take care of.* Look at the following:

> While Ronald was sick, his mother **looked after** him.
> While Ronald was sick, his mother *cared for* him.
> While Ronald was sick, his mother *took care of* him.

I'll see you later.[14]
Instead of saying *Good bye*, we can say **See you** or **See you later.** (For other alternatives, *see Language Notes 1-4-11, page 9.*)

♪➋🎥
10 - 5. Student Exercises: Fill in the blanks.
       Choose the best sentence from the list on the next page.

1	**Scott:**	How do you like my new *rollerblades*?
2	**Brennan:**	[ ]
3	**Scott:**	Ice-skates? [ ]
4	**Brennan:**	Gee. [ ] When did you buy them?
5	**Scott:**	Ah . . . [ ]
6	**Brennan:**	Can you skate, yet?
7	**Scott:**	Yeah, a little bit. [ ]
8	**Brennan:**	Be careful! You're still learning, so take it easy.
9	**Scott:**	Oh. I can't stop. Ah! [ ]
10	**Brennan:**	Ouch! That hurt! [ ]
11	**Scott:**	Sorry. I'm still learning.
12	**Brennan:**	Practice more, Scott. [ ]

Choose the best sentences for the blanks.
a) Watch out, Brennan!   e) See you later.
b) Watch this!   f) Have a closer look.
c) They look like ice-skates!   g) They look really cool.
d) Let me see . . . I got them last   h) You should look where you're
     week.   going!

10 - 6. Student Exercise: Select the best answer.

1.   Which sentence is bad?
       (a)   That looks good!   (b)   This pie tastes great!
       (c)   That sounds terrible!   (d)   All sentences are okay.

2.   **Take a look** is the same as:
       (a)   Take a see.   (b)   Have a look.
       (c)   Take a watch.   (d)   Look like.

3.   Which sentence is bad?
      (a)   He looks like a girl.   (b)   It looks like snow.
      (c)   You look like crazy.   (d)   She looks like my wife.

4.   Instead of saying **Um . . .** or **Ah . . .** , we can say:
      (a)   Let me watch.   (b)   Let me look.
      (c)   Let me look out.   (d)   Let me see.

5.   Instead of saying **search**, we can say:
      (a)   Look like.   (b)   Look for.
      (c)   Look at.   (d)   Look out.

6.   **Watch out** is the same as:
      (a)   Look out.   (b)   See out.
      (c)   Watch this.   (d)   Look for.

7.   **I have to see the doctor** usually means:
      (a)   I have to hunt the doctor.   (b)   I have to look at the doctor.
      (c)   I have to visit the doctor.   (d)   I have to watch the doctor.

8.   Instead of saying **I understand**, we can say:
      (a)   I see.   (b)   I look.
      (c)   I watch.   (d)   I search.

9.   **Take care of . . .** or **Care for . . .** are the same as:
      (a)   Look for.   (b)   Look after.
      (c)   Take watch.   (d)   See care.

10.   *Rollerblades*™ are:
      (a)   Inline skates.   (b)   Indoor skates.
      (c)   Ice skates.   (d)   Skateboards.

10 - 7. Review of this lesson's major points. Do you understand these
         sentences, expressions and words?

Inline skates	Look	Look like	Look after
Inline skater	Taste	Taste like	Take care of
Rollerblades™	Sound	Sound like	Care for
Rollerblader™	Smell	Smell like	Look for
See you.	Feel	Feel like	See (meet/visit)
Let me see. . .	Take a look	Look out	See
I see.	Have a look	Watch out	Watch this!

10 - 8. Student Exercise: Can you help Hobbyman?
    Hobbyman wants to try rollerblading. Can you help him get from the
    left side of the puzzle to the right side of the puzzle? Target time is
    thirty seconds. Good luck!

10 - 9. Student Exercise: On the next page is a list of skating words. Can you
    find all of them in the word search below? Words are hidden horizontally -
    (left to right), vertically - (top to bottom) and diagonally - (top left to
    bottom right). Target time is **two minutes**.

S	H	O	B	B	Y	M	A	N	L	M	W	U
B	E	A	R	I	N	G	S	T	A	M	R	S
W	H	E	E	L	S	W	Z	D	C	P	I	I
S	T	O	P	P	E	R	X	S	E	P	S	D
F	W	F	S	K	A	T	E	R	S	H	T	K
V	J	U	B	O	O	T	S	R	I	E	G	N
S	P	E	E	D	M	E	B	O	L	L	U	E
Z	Y	Y	I	A	I	R	B	L	A	M	A	E
I	N	L	I	N	E	Q	V	L	H	E	R	D
S	K	A	T	E	S	F	T	E	A	T	D	P
W	T	R	A	N	S	P	O	R	T	D	E	A
B	U	C	K	L	E	O	U	C	H	J	E	D
O	Q	L	N	E	L	B	O	W	P	A	D	S

Air	Elbowpad	Laces	Speed
Bearings	Helmet	Ouch	Stopper
Blades	Hobbyman	Roller	Transport
Boots	Inline	Skater	Wheels
Buckle	Kneepads	Skates	Wristguard

10 - 10. Student Exercise: STEREOGRAM. Can you see the hidden answer?

Brennan: When were roller skates first invented, anyway?
Scott: Don't you know?
Brennan: No. I have no idea.
Scott: Well . . . they were invented in New York in (. . . . .).

To find out when roller skates were invented, please look at this stereogram :

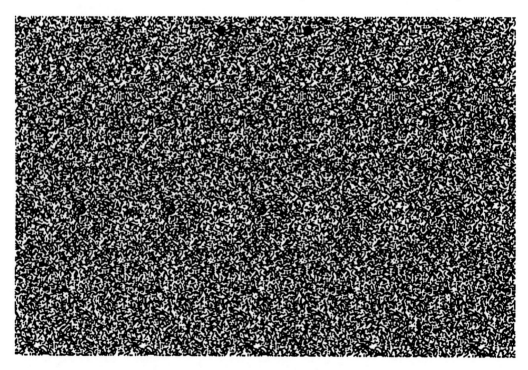

When were roller skates first invented?_____

10 - 11. Student exercise: How well did you understand the first dialogue?
Answer the following questions with **true** (T) or **false** (F). Circle the
correct answer.

1.   The skater's name is Bill.   (T) or (F)

2. *Rollerblades*™ look like ice skates. (T) or (F)

3. *Rollerblades*™ aren't cheap. (T) or (F)

4. The skater paid $130 for his *Rollerblades*™. (T) or (F)

5. The skater hits a small tree. (T) or (F)

6. The skater loses his glasses after hitting the tree. (T) or (F)

7. The skater hurts his arm when he hits the tree. (T) or (F)

8. Hobbyman can't find the skater's glasses. (T) or (F)

9. The skater's sister will look after him. (T) or (F)

10. *Rollerblades*™ were invented by a 20 year old American. (T) or (F)

NOTES:

DID YOU KNOW THAT ...

Did you know that *angling* means catching fish with a rod and line. *Fishing* means catching fish in any way - for example, by net or spear. Most sport fishermen are *anglers*. Most professionsl fishermen, (people who catch fish as their work), do not use a rod and line. The first *angling* book was written by a woman, in 1496, nearly 500 years ago. Nowadays, *angling*, often called fishing, is a very popular sport or hobby all over the world.

11: FISHING

LESSON FOCUS: "ALMOST/ NEARLY/ JUST ABOUT"

♫㉒🎥

11 - 1. Dialogue: Hobbyman meets an angler.

1	**Hobbyman:**	Hi there! Are the fish biting, today?
2	**Angler:**	I've caught one or two.
3	**Hobbyman:**	Do you go fishing every Sunday?
4	**Angler:**	Yeah. <u>I go fishing on almost every Sunday.</u>[1]
5	**Hobbyman:**	But it's 5 in the morning! Do you always get up so early?
6	**Angler:**	Well, <u>nearly all fishermen get up early.</u>[2] <u>Almost nobody catches any fish if they come late.</u>[3]
7	**Hobbyman:**	And you always catch fish?
8	**Angler:**	<u>Well, almost always.</u>[4]
9	**Hobbyman:**	How long do you usually fish?
10	**Angler:**	About 2 or 3 hours. <u>I'm almost finished for today.</u>[5]
11	**Hobbyman:**	Tell me about your biggest fish.
12	**Angler:**	Well, <u>almost one year ago, I was fishing here.</u>[6] It was <u>just about sunrise.</u>[7] Suddenly, I hooked a huge fish!
13	**Hobbyman:**	A huge fish? Was it very strong?
14	**Angler:**	Oh, yes. It was very strong. <u>It almost got away.</u>[8] In fact, <u>it nearly pulled me in the river.</u>[9]
15	**Hobbyman:**	What about today? Did you get any big fish?
16	**Angler:**	<u>I almost caught another large fish,</u>[10] but it got away. <u>Most of the fish that I caught today are pretty small.</u>[11]
17	**Hobbyman:**	<u>What is the most important thing in fishing?</u>[12]
18	**Angler:**	Well - <u>most guys say that good bait is the most important.</u>[13] I think that the rod, reel, hook, line and sinker are also important.
19	**Hobbyman:**	I see. Well, thanks for your time. I have to go now. I'll see you around.
20	**Angler:**	Okay. Goodbye.

11 - 2. Short Dialogues: More **"almost/just about/nearly"** sentences.

A: Do all Japanese have black hair?
B: Well . . . nearly all Japanese have black hair.

*   *   *

A: How often do you go fishing?
B: Just about every weekend.

*   *   *

A: Can you play the bagpipes?
B: Bagpipes? Almost nobody can play the bagpipes!

*   *   *

A: Can anybody learn to play golf?
B: Well . . . just about anybody can learn to play golf, I think.

*   *   *

A: Do you always drink beer every night, before going to bed?
B: Yeah, almost always.

*   *   *

A: Have you finished yet?
B: I've almost finished.

*   *   *

A: Hurry up? Aren't you ready?
B: Just a minute! I'm nearly ready.

*   *   *

A: Have you got the time?
B: Sure. It's almost 6 o'clock.

*   *   *

A: What time do the pubs open?
B: At 6pm, I think.
A: It's almost 6 now. Let's go!

*   *   *

A: Your face looks very pale.
B: I nearly had a car accident!

*   *   *

A: Are you married?
B: No, but I almost got married last year.

*   *   *

A: Can all of your friends drive?
B: Not all, but most of my friends can drive.

*   *   *

A: Who do you think is the most beautiful girl in the world?
B: Me!

*   *   *

A: Are all married men happy?
B: Most married men are happy.

*   *   *

A: Do you always read books?
B: Yeah, most of the time.

*   *   *

A: Almost all guys like girls.
B: And most girls like guys.

*   *   *

11 - 3. New Vocabulary: Do you know these words?

Angler: An **angler** is *a fisherman* that uses *a fishing rod and line.*
Angling: **Angling** means *fishing with a rod and line.*
Bait: **Bait** means *food that we can use to catch a fish. (See p.104)*
Float: A **float** is tied to a fishing line, so the hook *won't touch the bottom.*
 (See p.104)
Hook: A **hook** is tied to the end of a fishing line, so we can catch fish.
Huge: **Huge** means very big.
Line: **Line** means *fishing line. (See p.104)*
Pale: **Pale** means *a very light colour.* e.g. **You look pale**!
Pub: **Pub** means *public house* or *bar, - a drinking place.*
Reel: A **reel** holds the fishing line. *(See p.104)*
Rod: **Rod** means *fishing rod. (See p.104)*
Sinker: A **sinker** is *a heavy weight*, usually made of *lead. (See p.104)*

11 - 4. Language Notes: Language Notes

I go fishing on almost every Sunday.[1]
Almost, nearly and **just about** are the same. They have many uses. We often use these words with *all, every, no, none* or *any.* Look at the following diagram very carefully:
We are talking about *boys.*

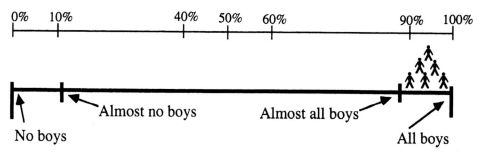

On the right side are *all boys*. On the left side are *no boys*. **Almost** *all boys* means *about 90% of boys*. **Almost** *no boys* means *about 10% of boys*. Look at the following examples:

Almost/nearly/just about		Meaning
I go fishing on **almost** every Sunday.	→	I go fishing most Sundays - *not every Sunday, but usually.*
Nearly all fishernmen get up early.	→	*Most* fishermen get up early - (maybe 90%) *not all, but most.*
Almost nobody catches fish if they come late.	→	*Most* people who come late *cannot* catch fish.

Nearly all fishermen get up early.[2]
Nearly all fishermen get up early means *Most fishermen get up early*. (*See Language Note 1*). **NOTE: Almost** *is not* the same as *most*. **Almost all** *is* the same as *most*.

Almost nobody catches any fish if they come late.[3]
Almost nobody catches any fish if they come late means *Most people who come late can not catch any fish*. (*See Language Note 1*).

Well, almost always.[4]
Almost always means *usually*. Look at the following diagram.

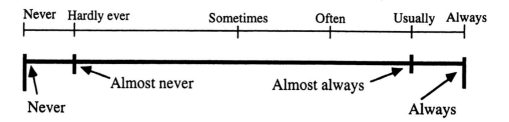

In the same way, **almost never** means *hardly ever* or *rarely*.

I'm almost finished for today.[5]
Almost, just about or **nearly** can also mean that *an action has almost finished*, or *a change has been completed*. Look at the following diagram:

I'm almost finished means *I will be finished soon*.

He's almost dead means *He will be dead soon* or *He is close to death*.

Almost one year ago, I was fishing here.[6] **It was just about sunrise.**[7]
We can also talk about time in the same way. **Almost one year ago** means *about one year ago* or *just under one year ago*. **It was just about sunrise** means *It was about sunrise*.   (*Look at the diagram on page 109.*)

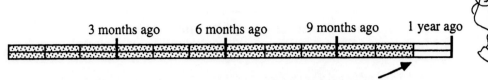

3 months ago   6 months ago   9 months ago   1 year ago

Almost one year ago

It almost got away.[8]

Almost, just about and **nearly** can also mean that *an action looked like being completed, but was not completed.* Look at the diagram:

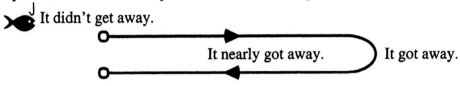

It didn't get away.

It didn't get away.

In this case, the fish **almost** got away. That means, *we thought the fish would escape, but it didn't.*

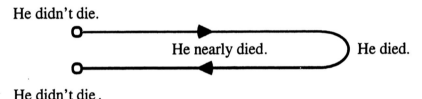

He didn't die.

In this case, he **nearly** died. That means, *we thought he would die, but he didn't.*   **Note: Always** use past tense in this type of sentence.

It nearly pulled me in the river.[9]

It nearly pulled me in the river means *I thought it might pull me in the river, but it didn't.*   (*See Language Note 8*)

I almost caught another large fish.[10]

I almost caught another large fish means *I thought I would catch another big fish, but I couldn't.*   (*See Language Note 8*)

Most of the fish that I caught today are pretty small.[11]

Most sometimes needs to use **of**. For example, if we use **the, these, that, my, your, his** etc, we *must* use **of**. Look at the following examples.

Most of my friends are girls.	He took **most of our** money.
Most of his hair is grey.	I've seen **most of this** movie.

Most guys say that good bait is the most important.[13]

If we don't use **the, these, that, my, your, his** etc, we don't need **of**.

Most foreigners like sushi.	I like **most** beers.
Most people like travelling.	They have been to **most** countries.

Never say **Most <u>of</u> foreigners like sushi** or **I like most <u>of</u> beers**, etc.

<u>What is the most important thing in fishing?</u>[12]

The most can also be used with adjectives over 2 syllables, (e.g. dif-fi-cult, in-ter-est-ing, dan-ger-ous etc), and nouns.

Adjectives: ➡	I think America is **the most** dangerous country.
	She is **the most** beautiful girl that I've ever met.
Nouns: ➡	He has **the most** money in the world.
	I have **the most** CD's in my class.

♫⓭🎥

11 - 5. Student Exercises: Fill in the blanks.
Choose the best sentence from the list at the bottom of this page.

1 **John Dory:** G'day Gill. I didn't know you were an angler.
2 **Gill:** Really? [   ]
3 **John Dory:** Everyday? [   ]
4 **Gill:** Yeah. [   ]
5 **John Dory:** [   ]
6 **Gill:** Usually 2 or 3 hours. [   ]
7 **John Dory:** Did you catch any big fish today?
8 **Gill:** Not really. [   ]
9 **John Dory:** Haven't you ever caught a big fish?
10 **Gill:** No. [   ]
11 **John Dory:** I see. Anyway, I gotta' go now. I'll call you at home.
12 **Gill:** At home? [   ] I'm always fishing.

Choose the best sentences for the blanks.

a) I almost always catch 1 or 2.
b) I'm almost never at home.
c) Most of today's fish are pretty small.
d) How long do you fish for, on most days?
e) I go fishing nearly everyday!
f) I've just about finished for today.
g) But I almost caught a big one last week.
h) Do you catch fish, most of the time?

11 - 6. Student Exercise: Select the best answer.

1. **Nearly** is the same as:
    (a) Nearby.   (b) Near.
    (c) Most.   (d) Just about.

2. **Almost all** is the same as:
    (a) Most.   (b) Just about.
    (c) Nearly.   (d) Mostly.

3. **Usually** is the same as:
    (a) Almost never.   (b) Just about always.
    (c) Sometimes.   (d) Nearly all.

4. **He is almost ready** means:
    (a) He is ready.   (b) He is not ready.
    (c) He'll be ready soon.   (d) He is always ready.

5. **Just about 3 months ago** means:
    (a) More than 3 months ago. (b) Probably 3 months ago.
    (c) Most of 3 months ago.   (d) About 3 months ago.

6. You play a game of basketball. Your team has the most points and you
    think your team will win. Suddenly, one minute before the game ends,
    the other team wins. Your team loses, but you can say:
    (a) We most won.   (b) We just won.
    (c) We almost always win. (d) We nearly won.

7. Which sentence is bad?
    (a) Most of Japanese men   (b) Most of the girls I know can
         like golf.   speak a foreign language.
    (c) Most of his ideas are bad.(d) Most of my friends don't smoke.

8. Which sentence is good?
    (a) Most drivers never drink.(b) Most fish live in the sea.
    (c) Paul can play most   (d) All sentences are okay.
         instruments.

9. Which sentence is bad?
    (a) He has the most   (b) Simon is the most handsome
         powerful computer.   guy in our class.
    (c) The whale is the most   (d) I think bungy jumping is the most
         big fish in the sea.   dangerous sport in the world.

10. Which 3 words are the same?
    (a) (just about, most, almost)(b) (almost, nearly, just about)
    (c) (almost, about, nearly) (d) (nearly, most, just about)

11 - 7. Review of this lesson's major points. Do you understand these words, sentences and expressions?

Angler	Almost	It almost got away.
Angling	Just about	He nearly died.
Bait	Nearly	I just about wet my pants.
Float	Almost every	Most of the fish
Hook	Nearly all	Most of our money
Huge	Just about no	Most of his hair
Line	Almost anyone	Most of this movie
Pale	Almost always	Most beers
Pub	Just about never	Most people
Reel	Almost finished	The most important thing
Rod	Just about ready	The most difficult song
Sinker	Almost one year ago	The most money
	Just about sunrise	The most CDs

11 - 8. Student exercise: Spot the difference.
Look at the illustration on page 104. There are 5 differences between the top and bottom illustrations. Please describe the differences in the space below. (Hint: You should begin *In the top picture, there is . . .*   or   *In the bottom picture, Hobbyman has . . .*   etc)

(i)   _____

(ii)   _____

(iii)   _____

(iv)   _____

(v)   _____

11 - 9. Student exercise: How well did you understand the first dialogue? Answer the following questions with **true** (T) or **false** (F). Circle the correct answer.

1.   The angler's name is Gill.   (T) or (F)

2.   The angler has caught one or two fish.   (T) or (F)

3.   The angler rarely goes fishing on Sunday.   (T) or (F)

4.   Almost all fishermen get up early.   (T) or (F)

5.   Almost everybody catches a fish if they come late.   (T) or (F)

6.   The angler usually fishes for 3 or 4 hours.   (T) or (F)

7.   The angler hooked a huge fish nearly 2 years ago at sunrise.   (T) or (F)

8.   Most guys say that good bait is the most important thing in
      fishing.   (T) or (F)

9.   The angler thinks that the rod, reel, line, hook and sinker   (T) or (F)
      aren't very important for fishing.

10.   The first angling book was written by a woman in 1946.   (T) or (F)

NOTES:

DID YOU KNOW THAT ...

Did you know that the first steam-powered automobile was made in France in 1769. In 1885, *Karl Benz* made the first gasoline powered motor car. In 1895, the first car race was held in America. The first Grand Prix was held in France, in 1906. Henry Ford began making cheap cars (*called the Model T Ford*) in 1908. The first Nissan was made in 1917, and the first Toyota was built in 1935. In 1992, 47 377 334 cars were built in various countries. Just over 25% were built in Japan!

12: CARS

LESSON FOCUS: NUMBERS

♪㉔🎥

12 - 1. Dialogue: Hobbyman meets a car-lover.

1	**Hobbyman:**	Hello. I like your car.
2	**Car-lover:**	Thanks. I love cars. By the way, my name's John. Nice to meet you.
3	**Hobbyman:**	Nice to meet you, too. I'm Hobbyman. Umm . . could you tell me about your car?
4	**Car-lover:**	Sure, it's a '93 model (*ninety three*) Cherokee.[1]
5	**Hobbyman:**	How much did it cost?
6	**Car-lover:**	In America, it costs about 25 *thou*,[2] but I bought it in Japan. It was about 4 000 000 (*four million*) yen.[3]
7	**Hobbyman:**	4 *mil*![4] That sounds expensive!
8	**Car-lover:**	Oh . . . it was about 3.8 million (*three point eight million*) plus tax.[5]
9	**Hobbyman:**	Is it economical?
10	**Car-lover:**	Oh . . . it does about 6.3 km/l (*six point three kilometres per litre*),[6] or 19½ (*nineteen and a half*) miles per gallon.[7]
11	**Hobbyman:**	I see. What is the top speed?
12	**Car-lover:**	Top speed is about 190 (*one ninety*).[8]
13	**Hobbyman:**	Wow! What did you drive before this?
14	**Car-lover:**	Ah, I had a Benz 190 (*one ninety*).[9] And I also had a Honda 250 (*two fifty*).
15	**Hobbyman:**	Do you have any other cars now?
16	**Car-lover:**	I have a 1908 (*nineteen oh eight*) T Model Ford.[10] If you want to see it, please give me a call. My number is 551-2333 (*double five one two triple three*).[11] I have a driving lesson at 6:05 (*six oh five*),[12] so please call before then.
17	**Hobbyman:**	Okay. Thanks for showing me your car, John.
18	**Car-lover:**	No problem, Hobbyman. See ya' around.
19	**Hobbyman:**	Okay. Bye John.

12 - 2. Short Dialogues: More "**number**" sentences.

A: What sort of car is that?
B: It's a '39 model Ford.

*   *   *

A: How much was your new house?
B: Including tax, about 140 *thou.*

*   *   *

A: How many people are there in Australia?
B: About 18 000 000, I think.

*   *   *

A: How much will the bridge cost?
B: I'm not sure. Maybe 2 or 3 *mil.*

*   *   *

A: How many Toyota Corollas have been made?
B: I think, almost 1.7 million.

*   *   *

A: How big is your car engine?
B: It's 2.6 litres. (*two point six*)

*   *   *

A: Is your car very economical, or is it a gas guzzler?
B: It's economical - 9 km/l. (*nine kilometres per litre*)

*   *   *

A: How many pizzas did you eat?
B: I ate $3\frac{2}{3}$. (*three and two thirds*)

*   *   *

A: What's the top speed?
B: About 180. (*one eighty*)

*   *   *

A: What car do you drive?
B: A Nissan 180. (*one eighty*)

*   *   *

A: What size is your bike?
B: I've got a Honda 750. (*seven fifty*)

*   *   *

A: How tall are you?
B: I'm about 180. (*one eighty*)

*   *   *

A: When were you born?
B: I was born in 1903. (*nineteen oh three*)

*   *   *

A: Have you got the time?
B: It's 9.02. (*nine oh two*)

*   *   *

A: What's your phone number?
B: My number is 522- 4440. (*five double two, triple four oh*)

*   *   *

A: Is that your third drink?
B: No. It's my ninth drink!

*   *   *

12 - 3. New Vocabulary: Do you know these words?

Automobile:	**Automobile** means *car*.
Economical:	An **economical** car can travel a long way *using only a small amount of gasoline.*
Gas-guzzler:	A **gas-guzzler** is the opposite of an **economical** car. **Guzzle** means *drink*, so a **gas-guzzler** *drinks gasoline.*
Mil:	*Mil* is the short form of **million** (*in conversation*).
Motor car:	**Motor car** means *car*.
Thou:	*Thou* is the short form of **thousand** (*in conversation*).
Vehicle:	**Vehicle** means *car, truck, bike* or *bus* etc.

12 - 4. Language Notes: Language Notes

It's a '93 model (*ninety three*) Cherokee.[1]

We often shorten years to the last two numbers, in daily conversation. Look at the following examples:

In the summer of **'63**, I first came to America. →	In the summer of *1963*, I first came to America.
She was born in **'55**. →	She was born in *1955*.
I bought a **'63** Corvette. →	I bought a *1963* Corvette.

It was about 4 000 000 (*four million*) yen.[3]

The English number system is easy to understand. Look at the following diagram very carefully:

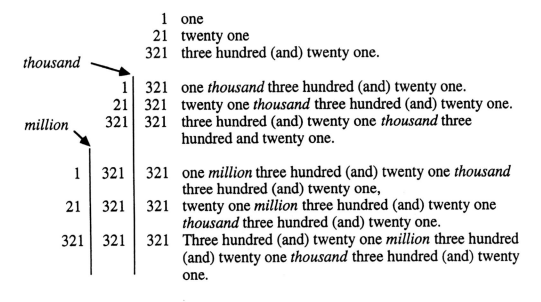

		1	one
		21	twenty one
		321	three hundred (and) twenty one.
thousand	1	321	one *thousand* three hundred (and) twenty one.
	21	321	twenty one *thousand* three hundred (and) twenty one.
million	321	321	three hundred (and) twenty one *thousand* three hundred and twenty one.
1	321	321	one *million* three hundred (and) twenty one *thousand* three hundred (and) twenty one,
21	321	321	twenty one *million* three hundred (and) twenty one *thousand* three hundred (and) twenty one.
321	321	321	Three hundred (and) twenty one *million* three hundred (and) twenty one *thousand* three hundred (and) twenty one.

Also look at the following:

3 000 000	3	**Million**
30 000 000	30	**Million**
300 000 000	300	**Million**
3 000 000 000	3	**Billion**
3 000 000 000 000	3	**Trillion**

4 *mil!*[4] In America, it costs about 25 *thou.*[2]

In conversation, **million** is often shortened to *mil*. In the same way, **thousand** is often shortened to *thou*. Look at the following:

How many people are there in Japan? I'm not sure. About 130 *million*.	→ How many people are there in Japan? → I'm not sure. About 130 *mil*.
How much did you win? Almost 2 *million* dollars!!	→ How much did you win? → Almost 2 *mil*!!

Note: If we shorten **2 million** *dollars* or **2 million** *people*, usually we only say **2 mil**. We don't have to say *dollars* or *people*.

It was about 3.8 million (*three point eight million*) plus tax.[5]

With large numbers, (*more than one million*), we often use *a decimal point*. This is quicker and easier to understand. For example:

There are over *5 710 000* (*five million seven hundred thousand*) people in Hong Kong.	There are over **5.71 million** → (*five point seven one million*) people in Hong Kong.

Sometimes we *round off* the number to make it easier to understand.

Australia's area is *7 686 810* (*seven million six hundred and eighty six thousand eight hundred and ten*) square kilometres.	Australia's area is **about** → **7.7 million** (*seven point seven million*) square kilometres.

It does about 6.3 km/l (*six point three kilometres per litre*).[6]

The mark "/" is read **per**. Look at the following examples:

km/l	kilometres **per** litre
m/s	metres **per** second
km/h	kilometres **per** hour

19 $\frac{1}{2}$ *(nineteen and a half)* **miles per gallon.**[7]
Fractions are easy to read:

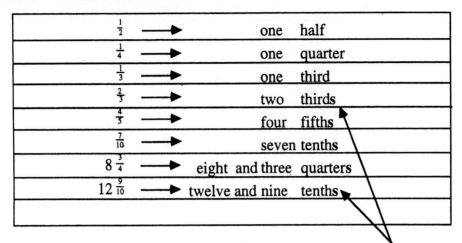

$\frac{1}{2}$ ⟶	one	half
$\frac{1}{4}$ ⟶	one	quarter
$\frac{1}{3}$ ⟶	one	third
$\frac{2}{3}$ ⟶	two	thirds
$\frac{4}{5}$ ⟶	four	fifths
$\frac{7}{10}$ ⟶	seven	tenths
$8\frac{3}{4}$ ⟶	eight and three	quarters
$12\frac{9}{10}$ ⟶	twelve and nine	tenths

Note: If fractions have more than one part, the letter "s" is needed.

Top speed is about 190 *(one ninety)*.[8] **I had a Benz 190 .**[9]
Numbers with three or four digits are *often* read a special way. For example:

What's the top speed?	160 km/h.	*(one sixty)*
How tall are you?	185 cm.	*(one eighty five)*
How long are your skis?	196 cm	*(one ninety six)*
What model is your car?	Benz 190	*(one ninety)*
What room are you in?	Room 1520	*(fifteen twenty)*
What time is it now?	7.45	*(seven forty five)*
How much do you weigh?	220 pounds	*(two twenty)*
What is your best marathon time?	2hrs 30mins	*(two thirty)*

In these cases, we only have to say the number. (We don't need to say *cm*, *km/h*, *room number* etc.)

I have a 1908 *(nineteen oh eight)* **T Model Ford.**[10]
We can't *shorten* years that have the number *zero* in them. (*See Language Note 1.*) In such cases, we need to say the year completely, and the *zero* is pronounced **oh.** For example:

1906 - *nineteen oh six*	1804 - *eighteen oh four*

My number is 551-2333 *(double five one, two triple three)*.[11]
When saying phone numbers, we often say **double** or **triple.** Also, similar to years (*Language Note 10*), *zero* is usually pronounced **oh.** Look at the following examples:

881-3322	*double eight one, **double** three **double** two.*
611-0333	*six **double** one, oh **triple** three*
532-0040	*five three two, **double oh** four oh*

I have a driving lesson at 6:05 (*six oh five*).[12]

Similarly to years and phone numbers, when we tell the time, *zero* is also pronounced **oh**. Look at the diagram:

| 8:07 | *eight **oh** seven* | 8:07 | ~~*eight seven*~~ |

Don't forget to say **oh**!

♫㉕🎥

12 - 5. Student Exercises: Fill in the blanks.
         Choose the best sentence from the list on the next page.

1	**Henry:**	Hi Karl. They say you bought a new car.
2	**Karl:**	That's right. [＿＿＿＿＿＿＿＿＿]
3	**Henry:**	Nice car. What did that cost? [＿＿＿＿＿]
4	**Karl:**	No. I bought it second hand. [＿＿＿＿＿]
5	**Henry:**	It has a big engine, doesn't it? [＿＿＿＿]
6	**Karl:**	Yeah, it's not very economical. [＿＿＿＿＿]
7	**Henry:**	How old is it?
8	**Karl:**	[＿＿＿＿＿＿＿＿] Anyway, what's the time?
9	**Henry:**	[＿＿＿＿＿＿＿＿＿＿＿＿＿＿＿＿]
10	**Karl:**	Really! I gotta' go. I'll call you later. What's your number?
11	**Henry:**	[＿＿＿＿＿] Give me a call, and show me your car.
12	**Karl:**	Okay Henry. I'll call you. See ya'.

Choose the best sentences for the blanks.

a)	It only cost $40 000.	e)	70 or 80 thou?
b)	551-3330.	f)	I bought a Benz 560.
c)	Is it a gas-guzzler?	g)	It does about 5 km/l.
d)	It's 6:04.	h)	It's a '91 model.

12 - 6. Student Exercise: Select the best answer.

1.   In conversation, instead of saying **1965**, we often say:
   (a) Six five.   (b) One nine six five.
   (c) Oh six five.   (d) Sixty five.

2.   The number **8000000000** is read:
   (a) Eight million.   (b) Eighty million.
   (c) Eight hundred million. (d) Eight billion.

3. The short form of **two million dollars** is:
    (a)   Two *mil.*   (b)   Two *mil* dollars.
    (c)   Two *milli* dollars.   (d)   Two *milli.*

4. The short form of **5780000** is:
    (a)   Five hundred and   (b)   Five point seven eight
          seventy eight thousand.   million.
    (c)   Fifty seven point eight (d)   Point five seven eight
          million.   billion.

5. **km/l** means:
    (a)   Kilometres in litre.   (b)   Kilometres one litre.
    (c)   Kilometres every litre. (d)   Kilometres per litre.

6. The fraction $\left(\frac{2}{3}\right)$ is read:
    (a)   Two threes.   (b)   Two thirds.
    (c)   Two third.   (d)   Two three.

7. **1806** is read:
    (a)   Eighteen zero six.   (b)   Eighty six.
    (c)   Eighteen oh six.   (d)   Eighty oh six.

8. The answer is **One fifty**. What is the question?
    (a)   How tall are you?   (b)   What's your room number?
    (c)   What time is it now?   (d)   All sentences are okay.

9. My telephone number is **633-0001**. Which answer is the best?
    (a)   *Six double three, double* (b)   *Six triple three, double oh*
          oh one.   *one.*
    (c)   *Six triple three, triple* (d)   *Six double three, triple oh*
          zero one.   *one.*

10. The time is **8:05**. This is usually said as:
    (a)   Eight five.   (b)   Eight zero five.
    (c)   Eight past five.   (d)   Eight oh five.

12 - 7. Review of this lesson's major points. Do you understand these words
         and expressions?

Automobile	'93 model	*Thou*	160km/h
Economical	Million	*Mil*	220 pounds
Gas-guzzler	Billion	*Km/l*	11:05
Motor car	Trillion	$\frac{7}{10}$	1908
Vehicle	2.5 Million	$8\frac{1}{4}$	553-0003

12 - 8. Student Exercise: Complete the following Crossword.

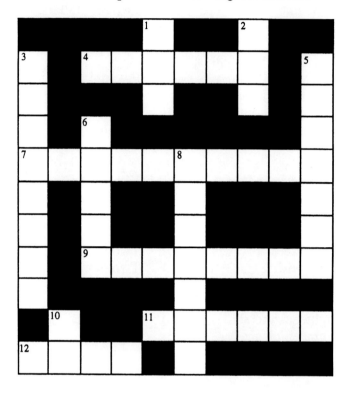

Across

4) **555-1234** can be read,
(_ _ _ _ _ _ five, one two three four.)

7) A car which doesn't use much gasoline is _ _ _ _ _ _ _ _ _ _ .

9) **1 000 000 000 000** is called one _ _ _ _ _ _ _ .

11) **532-1233** can be read, (five three two one two _ _ _ _ _ _ three).

12) The short form for one thousand (in conversation) is one _ _ _ _ .

Down

1) The short form for one million (in conversation) is one _ _ _ .

2) In "**km/l**", the "l" means _ _ _ .

3) The fraction $\frac{2}{7}$ is pronounced two _ _ _ _ _ _ _ _ .

5) **1 000 000 000** is called one _ _ _ _ _ _ _ .

6) **5.7** is read five _ _ _ _ _ seven.

8) **1 000 000** is called one _ _ _ _ _ _ _ .

10) **6:04** can be read six _ _ four.

12 - 9. Student Exercise: On the next page is a list of car words. Can you find all of them in the word search? (Also next page) Words are hidden horizontally - (left to right), vertically - (top to bottom) and diagonally - (top left to bottom right). Target time is **two minutes**.

```
Q  D  C  A  R  B  U  R  E  T  O  R  L  U
E  R  G  L  B  A  T  T  E  R  Y  D  W  F
V  G  W  L  U  V  M  G  D  A  N  O  I  L
M  E  F  I  M  T  G  G  S  N  Z  O  N  M
B  A  F  R  P  D  C  W  E  S  Q  R  D  K
H  R  W  R  E  E  W  H  A  M  T  Y  S  I
E  B  P  P  R  N  R  E  T  I  A  G  H  G
A  O  R  R  G  G  N  E  B  S  S  R  I  N
D  X  R  A  D  I  A  L  E  S  H  I  E  I
L  Z  S  Y  K  N  Y  K  L  I  T  L  L  T
A  C  C  E  L  E  R  A  T  O  R  L  D  I
M  X  F  F  A  N  T  E  N  N  A  E  B  O
P  S  H  I  F  T  H  O  B  B  Y  M  A  N
S  U  N  R  O  O  F  E  R  M  L  W  C  F
```

Accelerator	Carburetor	Hobbyman	Shift
Antenna	Clutch	Ignition	Sunroof
Ashtray	Engine	Oil	Transmission
Battery	Gearbox	Radial	Wheel
Brake	Grille	Seat	Windshield
Bumper	Headlamp	Seatbelt	Wiper

12 - 10. Student exercise: Did you understand the first dialogue? Answer the
following questions with **true** (T) or **false** (F). Circle the correct answer.

1.   The car-lover's name is Jim.   (T) or (F)

2.   He owns a '92 model Cherokee.   (T) or (F)

3.   In America, that car costs about $25 000.   (T) or (F)

4.   In Japan, it was about 3 000 000 yen.   (T) or (F)

5.   The Cherokee is very economical.   (T) or (F)

6.   It does about 6.3 km/l.   (T) or (F)

7.   It's top speed is about 210 km/h.   (T) or (F)

8.   Before, John had a Honda 250.   (T) or (F)

9.   He also owns a 1909 Model T Ford.   (T) or (F)

10.   Karl Benz made the first gasoline powered car in 1887.   (T) or (F)

DID YOU KNOW THAT . . .

Did you know that the first real bicycle was invented in Scotland in *1839*, by a 29 year old man. It weighed 26 kilograms. In *1868*, the first bicycle race was held in Paris. The distance was 2 kilometres. In *1870*, 2 Englishmen invented a lightweight, all-metal bicycle, with wire spoke wheels. The modern style rubber bicycle tyre was invented in *1888*. By *1896*, America's largest bicycle company was making one bike every minute! Now, bicycles are called *bikes*, are much lighter and faster, and are common all over the world.

13:
MOUNTAINBIKES

LESSON FOCUS: NEGATIVE QUESTIONS

♪㉖🎥

13 - 1. Dialogue: Hobbyman meets a mountain biker.

1	**Hobbyman:**	Hey, nice bike!
2	**Bike-rider:**	Yeah, thanks. My name's Dale, Dale Cannon.
3	**Hobbyman:**	I'm Hobbyman. Nice to meet you.
4	**Bike-rider:**	Good to meet you, too. I read about you in the papers. <u>You're not from Earth, are you?</u>[1]
5	**Hobbyman:**	No, I'm not.
6	**Bike-rider:**	<u>And people on your planet have many hobbies, don't they?</u>[2]
7	**Hobbyman:**	No, they don't. I came to Earth to learn about hobbies. May I ask you a few questions?
8	**Bike-rider:**	Sure.
9	**Hobbyman:**	Umm . . . <u>this isn't a mountain bike, is it?</u>[3]
10	**Bike-rider:**	Yes, it is. Look . . . it has smaller wheels, wider tyres, a stronger frame and more gears.
11	**Hobbyman:**	I see. <u>Mountain bikes are quite new, aren't they Dale?</u>[4]
12	**Bike-rider:**	Yes, they are. They became popular in the States in the late 70's. <u>You don't have any bikes on the planet Nohobby?</u>[5]
13	**Hobbyman:**	No, we don't. We fly everywhere. On this planet, <u>people usually just walk, right?</u>[6]
14	**Bike-rider:**	<u>That's right.</u>[7] For longer distances, we can catch a bus or taxi, drive a car, fly in a plane, maybe go by boat or ride a bike. I like bike riding because there's no pollution.
15	**Hobbyman:**	I've seen many cars, but bike riding doesn't seem so popular.
16	**Bike-rider:**	<u>That's correct,</u>[8] but it's getting a little more popular now, especially in the cities.
17	**Hobbyman:**	I see. Well, thanks for telling me about your hobby. I gotta' go now. See ya', Dale.
18	**Bike-rider:**	Okay. See ya', Hobbyman.

13 - 2. Short Dialogues: More questions and answers.

A: You <u>don't</u> like meat, <u>do you</u>?
B: <u>No, I don't</u>.

        *   *   *

A: He's <u>not</u> a policeman, <u>is he</u>?
B: <u>No, he's not</u>. He's a doctor.

        *   *   *

A: Your car's <u>not</u> new, <u>is it</u>?
B: <u>No, it's not</u>. It's 5 years old.

        *   *   *

A: He <u>can't</u> play tennis, <u>can he</u>?
B: <u>No, he can't</u>. He's hopeless.

        *   *   *

A: She <u>isn't</u> a teacher, <u>is she</u>?
B: <u>Yes, she is</u>.

        *   *   *

A: You <u>don't</u> like meat?
B: <u>No, I don't</u>.

        *   *   *

A: You <u>don't</u> like meat, <u>do you</u>?
B: <u>That's right</u>. <u>I don't</u>.

        *   *   *

A: She <u>won't</u> die, <u>will she</u>?
B: <u>That's correct</u>. <u>She won't</u>.

        *   *   *

A: You like meat, <u>don't you</u>?
B: <u>No, I don't</u>.

        *   *   *

A: He's a policeman, <u>isn't he</u>?
B: <u>No, he's not</u>. He's a doctor.

        *   *   *

A: Your car's new, <u>isn't it</u>?
B: <u>No, it's not</u>. It's 5 years old.

        *   *   *

A: He <u>can</u> play tennis, <u>can't he</u>?
B: <u>No, he can't</u>. He's hopeless.

        *   *   *

A: She's a teacher, <u>isn't she</u>?
B: <u>Yes, she is</u>.

        *   *   *

A: You like meat?
B: <u>Yes, I do</u>.

        *   *   *

A: You like meat, <u>don't you</u>?
B: <u>That's right</u>. <u>I do</u>.

        *   *   *

A: She <u>will</u> die, <u>won't she</u>?
B: <u>That's correct</u>. <u>She will</u>.

        *   *   *

13 - 3. New Vocabulary: Do you know these words?

Bikes: **Bikes** means *bicycles* or *motor bikes*. In this lesson, **bikes** means *bicycles*. (*Bicycle* is an not a common word in conversation.)

Hopeless: When we talk about people, **hopeless** means *unskilled* or *having no talent or ability*.

Pollution: **Pollution** means *waste, garbage or things bad for the environnment*. (e.g. *air pollution, water pollution* etc.)

The papers: **The papers** means *the newspapers*.

13 - 4. Language Notes: Language Notes

You're not from Earth, are you?[1] No, I'm not.

This is a *negative tag question* and a *negative* (or **No**) *answer*. The answer **agrees** with the question. Look at similar examples below.

1	You *don't* like beer, *do you?*	➡	**No**, I don't.
2	He *can't* sing very well, *can he?*	➡	**No**, he can't.
3	The weather *isn't* very nice, *is it?*	➡	**No**, it's not.
4	We *won't* sell our house, *will we?*	➡	**No**, we won't.

Don't worry about the question, or the tags. Only look at the answer. In example 1, **No, I don't** means *No, I don't like beer*. In example 2, **No, he can't** means *No, he can't sing very well*.

And people on your planet have many hobbies, don't they?[2] No, they don't.

This is a *positive tag question* and a *negative* (or **No**) *answer*. The answer **disagrees** with the question. Look at similar examples below.

1	You *like* beer, *don't you?*	➡	**No**, I don't.
2	He *can* sing very well, *can't he?*	➡	**No**, he can't.
3	The weather *is* very nice, *isn't it?*	➡	**No**, it's not.
4	We *will* sell our house, *won't we?*	➡	**No**, we won't.

Again, don't worry about the question, or the tags. Only look at the answer. In example 1, **No, I don't** means *No, I don't like beer*. In example 2, **No, he can't** means *No, he can't sing very well*. ***Compare Language Notes 1 & 2.***

1	You ***don't like*** beer, ***do you?*** You ***like*** beer, ***don't you?***	➡	**No**, I don't. **No**, I don't.
2	He ***can't*** sing very well, ***can he?*** He ***can*** sing very well, ***can't he?***	➡	**No**, he can't. **No**, he can't.

The questions are **different**, but the answers are the **same**.

This isn't a mountain bike, is it?[3] Yes, it is.

This is a *negative tag question* and a *positive* (or **Yes**) *answer*. The answer **disagrees** with the question. Look at similar examples below.

1	You *don't* like beer, *do you*?	→	**Yes**, I do.
2	He *can't* sing very well, *can he*?	→	**Yes**, he can.
3	The weather *isn't* very nice, *is it*?	→	**Yes**, it is.
4	We *won't* sell our house, *will we*?	→	**Yes**, we will.

Don't worry about the question, or the tags. Only look at the answer. In example 1, **Yes, I do** means *Yes, I do like beer*. In example 2, **Yes, he can** means *Yes, he can sing very well*.

Mountain bikes are quite new, aren't they Dale?[4] Yes, they are.

This is a *positive tag question* and a *positive* (or **Yes**) *answer*. The answer **agrees** with the question. Look at similar examples below.

1	You *like* beer, *don't you*?	→	**Yes**, I do.
2	He *can* sing very well, *can't he*?	→	**Yes**, he can.
3	The weather *is* very nice, *isn't it*?	→	**Yes**, it is.
4	We *will* sell our house, *won't we*?	→	**Yes**, we will.

Don't worry about the question, or the tags. Only look at the answer. In example 1, **Yes, I do** means *Yes, I do like beer*. In example 2, **Yes, he can** means *Yes, he can sing very well*.   ***Compare Language Notes 3 & 4:***

1	You ***don't*** like beer, ***do you***? You ***like*** beer, ***don't you***?	→	**Yes**, I do. **Yes**, I do.
2	He ***can't*** sing very well, ***can he***? He ***can*** sing very well, ***can't he***?	→	**Yes**, he can. **Yes**, he can.

The questions are **different**, but the answers are the **same**. Whether the *question* is *negative* or *positive*, the *answer* is the *same* - either **yes** or **no**. The question does not affect the answer.

You don't have any bikes on the planet Nohobby?[5]

In conversation, we can make a question by using a *negative* or *positive* sentence, with a rising intonation. Look at the following examples:

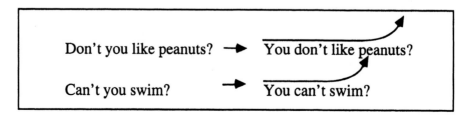

People usually just walk, right?[6]

Right can be used like a tag. If you say **right** on the end of a question, you want people to agree with you. **Right** is a short form of **That's right, isn't it.** (*See next Language Note*). We use **right?** with positive and negative sentences (*See Language Notes 5 & 6*), to make questions. We *don't* use **right** with normal questions. Look at the following examples:

You don't like him, **right**?	→	No. I can't stand him.
You're Ray Charles, **right**?	→	Yes, I am.
~~Don't you like him,~~ right?	→	No. I can't stand him.
~~Are you Ray Charles,~~ right?	→	Yes, I am.

That's right.[7] That's correct.[8]

When we agree with people, we can say **That's right** or **That's correct**. **That's right** or **That's correct** can both be used for *agreeing with a positive or negative question or sentence*. They can mean either **Yes** or **No**.

Yes	You like beer, don't you?		**That's right**. I love it!
	He's a really stupid guy.	→	**That's right** - really stupid!
	You're a doctor?		**That's correct**. Can I help you?
No	You can't swim, can you?		**That's right**. I'm hopeless.
	She's really clever!	→	**That's right**! She knows everything!
	You're not a nurse!		**That's correct**. I'm a cleaner.

Special Note: Sometimes "Negative tag questions" (Language Notes 1 & 3) can be used to show disbelief or surprise. For example, "You're not selling your car, are you?" means "Are you going to sell your car? I'm very surprised about that!"

♫ ㉗ 🎥

13 - 5. Student Exercises: Fill in the blanks.
Choose the best sentence from the list on the next page.

1	**Harley:**	Hey Dave. [?]
2	**David:**	[ ] My old one is broken.
3	**Harley:**	[?]
4	**David:**	[ ] I only bought it about 8 months ago.
5	**Harley:**	[?]
6	**David:**	No, I couldn't. The frame and the wheels are no good.
7	**Harley:**	I see. Will you buy a Japanese bike or an American bike?
8	**David:**	I'm not sure. Umm . . . Isn't your bike a Japanese bike?
9	**Harley:**	[ ] It's an American bike.
10	**David:**	[?]
11	**Harley:**	[ ] Anyway, it's getting late. I'd better go.
12	**David:**	Yeah, I've gotta' get out of here, too. See ya' later Harley.

Choose the best sentences for the blanks.

a)   It's new?   e)   No, it's not.
b)   Yes, it is.   f)   That's right.
c)   You could repair your old bike?g)   Yes, I am.
d)   Your old bike is less than 1   h)   You're not buying a new bike, are
     year old, isn't it?   you?

13 - 6. Student Exercise: Select the best answer.

1.   The question is **He's not a teacher, is he?** If you agree, you say:
     (a)   Yes, he is.   (b)   No, he is.
     (c)   Yes, he's not.   (d)   No, he's not.

2.   The question is **She's a pilot, isn't she?** If you disagree, you say:
     (a)   Yes, she is.   (b)   No, she is.
     (c)   Yes, she's not.   (d)   No, she's not.

3.   The question is **I can't sing very well, can I?** If you disagree, you say:
     (a)   Yes, you can.   (b)   No, you can.
     (c)   Yes, you can't.   (d)   No, you can't.

4.   The question is **It's very warm, isn't it?** If you agree, you say:
     (a)   Yes, it is.   (b)   No, it is.
     (c)   Yes, it isn't.   (d)   No, it isn't.

5.   Instead of saying **Don't you catch the bus?**, we can say:
     (a)   Don't you catch bus?   (b)   You don't catch the bus?
     (c)   Don't catch bus, do you? (d)   Catch the bus, isn't it?

6.   What is the short form of **You're Stevie Wonder! Isn't that right?**
     (a)   You're Stevie Wonder,   (b)   You're Stevie Wonder, are you
           isn't it?   alright?
     (c)   Stevie Wonder is right? (d)   You're Stevie Wonder, right?

7.   Which answer does NOT agree with **He's sick, isn't he?**
     (a)   Yes, he is.   (b)   Yes, he isn't.
     (c)   That's right.   (d)   That's correct.

8.   The question is **It was raining, wasn't it?** If you agree, you say:
     (a)   That's right!   (b)   Yes, it wasn't.
     (c)   No, it was.   (d)   All answers are okay.

9.   The question is **It was raining, wasn't it?** If you disagree, you say:
     (a)   That's right!   (b)   Yes, it wasn't.
     (c)   No, it was.   (d)   All answers are bad.

10. **Hopeless** means:
   (a) Very clever.   (b) Unskilled.
   (c) No dreams.   (d) Thoughtful.

13 - 7. Review of this lesson's major points. Do you understand these sentences questions and words?

Bikes	You don't, do you?	You do, don't you?	That's right.
Hopeless	You didn't, did you?	You did, didn't you?	That's correct.
Pollution	You aren't, are you?	You are, aren't you?	You don't …?
The papers	You weren't, were you?	You were, weren't you?	You do … ?
	You can't, can you?	You can, can't you?	You do, right?
	You won't, will you?	You will, won't you?	You don't, right?

13 - 8. Student Exercise: Below is a list of bike words. Can you find all of them in the word search below? Words are hidden horizontally - (left to right), vertically - (top to bottom) and diagonally - (top left to bottom right). Target time is **two minutes**.

```
P M O U N T A I N M H N U
S E A T F I W Q S P A O D
R A D B I C Y C L E N H B
T I L A B I K E K I D A E
I Y M O L S P O K E B N A
X D R V C F R A M E R D R
B M X E M K R O B W A L I
M U D G U A R D A I K E N
H J U W H E E L P D E B G
H E L M E T S T A N D A N
U C H A I N F O R K I R V
T O H O B B Y M A N T S O
R C R A N K G E A R S A A
```

Bearing	Fork	Hobbyman	Road
Bicycle	Frame	Lock	Seat
Bike	Gears	Mountain	Spoke
BMX	Handbrake	Mudguard	Stand
Chain	Handlebars	Pedal	Tyre
Crank	Helmet	Rim	Wheel

13 - 9. Student Exercise: STEREOGRAM. Can you see the hidden answer?

Bill: When was the first real bicycle invented?
Ben: That's easy. 1839!
Bill: Very good! What was the average bike price in 1896 in the USA?
Ben: Wow! That's a hard one. Maybe about (. . . . .) .

To find out the average bike price in 1896, please look at this stereogram :

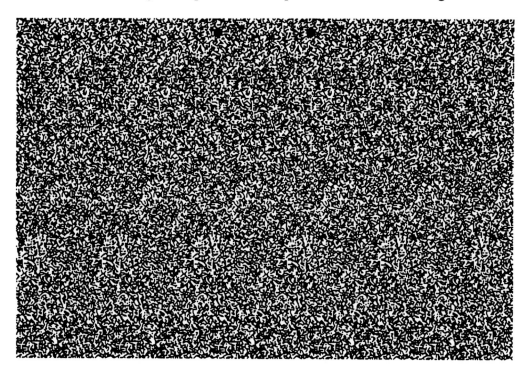

What was the average bike price in 1896?_____

13 - 10. Student exercise: How well did you understand the first dialogue?
Answer the following questions with **true** (T) or **false** (F). Circle the
correct answer.

1.   The mountain biker's name is Dale Canyon.   (T) or (F)

2.   Dale read about Hobbyman in the papers.   (T) or (F)

3.   A mountain bike has larger wheels and wider tyres.   (T) or (F)

4.   Mountain bikes are new.   (T) or (F)

5.   They became popular in the States in the 1960's.   (T) or (F)

6. There are many bikes on the planet Nohobby. (T) or (F)

7. On the planet Nohobby, people fly everywhere. (T) or (F)

8. Bike riding causes much pollution. (T) or (F)

9. Bike riding is not very popular now, especially in the cities. (T) or (F)

10. The first real bike weighed 28 kilograms. (T) or (F)

NOTES:

couch (sofa)

OID YOU KNOW THAT ...

Did you know that a couch potato is a person who spends much time sitting or lying down, usually watching television. The expression *couch potato* was originally American slang, but is now used in all English speaking countries, and has even entered some foreign languages, such as Japanese. Speaking of potatoes, did you also know that the largest potato in the world was grown in England in 1982. It weighed 3.2 kilograms!

14:
COUCHPOTATO

LESSON FOCUS : the verbs "COME & GO"

♫ ㉘ 🎥

14 - 1. Dialogue: Hobbyman meets a couch potato.

1	**Hobbyman:**	Hello! <u>May I come in?</u>[1]
2	**Couch Potato:**	Who are you?
3	**Hobbyman:**	I'm Hobbyman. <u>I come from Nohobby and . . .</u>[2]
4	**Couch Potato:**	<u>Go away!</u>[3]
5	**Hobbyman:**	I beg your pardon?
6	**Couch Potato:**	<u>Come on!</u>[4] Give me a break! <u>Go back home!</u>[5] I'm tired.
7	**Hobbyman:**	Huh?
8	**Couch Potato:**	<u>I want to go to sleep.</u>[6]
		(*A pretty girl comes into the room.*)[7]
9	**Girl-friend:**	Hey! You! <u>Come here!</u>[8]
10	**Hobbyman:**	Ah . . . okay.
11	**Girl-friend:**	Who are you and <u>what's going on?</u>[9]
12	**Hobbyman:**	I'm Hobbyman and I'm asking people about their hobbies.
13	**Girl-friend:**	My boyfriend hasn't got a hobby.
14	**Hobbyman:**	He's your boyfriend?
15	**Girl-friend:**	Yeah . . . <u>we've been going out for six years.</u>[10] He just likes lying on the sofa.
16	**Hobbyman:**	I see. Umm . . . May I ask you a few questions?
17	**Hobbyman:**	Sure, <u>go ahead.</u>[11]
18	**Hobbyman:**	You said that your boyfriend liked lying on the sofa. Is he sick, or <u>has he come down with a cold?</u>[12]
19	**Girl-friend:**	No. He just likes sitting on the sofa. He's a couch potato.
20	**Hobbyman:**	A couch potato? Is he lazy?
21	**Girl-friend:**	Yeah. <u>He never goes anywhere.</u>[13]
22	**Hobbyman:**	So, his hobby is doing nothing, right?
23	**Girl-friend:**	Yeah - I guess that's right!

14 - 2.   Short Dialogues: More "**come/go**" sentences.

A: Hello! May I come in?
B: Sure! Come in and sit down.

*   *   *

A: Where are you from?
B: Australia. How 'bout you?
A: I come from Vancouver, Canada.

*   *   *

A: Excuse me. May I ask you a few
         questions?
B: No! I'm busy! Go away!

*   *   *

A: Which horse do you want to win?
B: I really want number 5 to win.
         Come on, number 5! Come on!

*   *   *

A: Could you please lend me $10?
B: I'm sorry. I don't lend money.
A: Come on! I really need $10.

*   *   *

A: Come on! It's already 8pm!
B: Sorry, but I can't drive any faster!

*   *   *

A: When are you going back to Bali?
B: Probably in the spring, next year.

*   *   *

A: Please don't go to sleep now!
B: I'm tired. I can't stay awake.

*   *   *

A: Come to my office at 7:30.
B: Okay. I'll see you then.

*   *   *

A: Could you come here please?
B: Just a minute.
A: Come on! I'm waiting!

*   *   *

A: What's going on here?
B: We're preparing for a party
         tonight. 'You want to come?

*   *   *

A: How long have you been
         going out with her?
B: About 6 months, I think.

*   *   *

A: Would you mind if I lit a
         cigarette?
B: No problem! Go ahead.

*   *   *

A: What's wrong with you?
B: I've come down with the 'flu.

*   *   *

A: Did you go to the party?
B: Nah. I couldn't make it.

*   *   *

A: Do you think I'll win?
B: Go for it! Do your best!

*   *   *

14 - 3. New Vocabulary: Do you know these words?

Couch: A real **couch** means a long chair with a back and at least one arm rest. In conversation, **couch** means any type of long chair, such as a **sofa**, a **lounge**, a **divan**, a **settee** or a **chaise longue** etc.

Couch potato: A **couch potato** is a person who lays on a couch for a long time, usually watching TV.

14 - 4. Language Notes: Language Notes

May I come in?[1] **A pretty girl comes into the room.**[7]
Come in means *enter a room.* If you knock on someone's door, they will probably say **Come in.** You can also say **Can (May) I come in. Come into** also means *enter.*

I come from Nohobby and . . .[2]
When we talk about our home town, or where we were born, we often say **I'm from . . .** We can also say **I come from . . .** We *shouldn't* say **I came from . . .** because the meaning is different.

Go away![3]
In usual conversation, **Go away** has 2 different meanings. One meaning is *leave* (for a long time, or forever). e.g. **I have to go away to America.** The second meaning *is used as a command.* It means **Don't come near me.**

Come on![4]
Come on is a very useful expression in everyday conversation. It has 3 meanings. The first meaning is similar to *Hurry up.* The second meaning is *a form of encouragement.* The third meaning is *Please - I'm asking you or I'm requesting you.*

Hurry up	- It's already 7 o'clock. We going to be late. **Come on!** - You always walk so slow! **Come on!**
Encourage	- Hit a home run! **Come on!** A big hit, please! - You can do it! Shoot a goal! **Come on!**
Please - I'm asking you	- I don't want to drink anymore. **Come on!** Let's leave! - **Come on!** I'm tired. Let's talk about it later.

Remember, **Come on** does *not* mean **come here.**

Go back home![5] **Come here!**[8] **He never goes anywhere.**[13]
Go and **come** are basic words in English conversation, but are often confused. Look at the following diagrams:

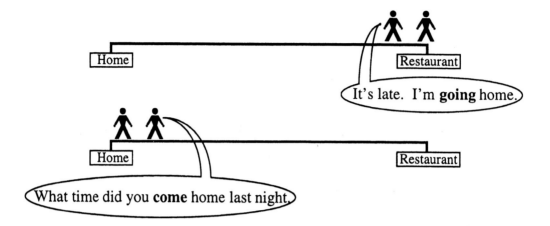

If we are at home when we speak, we can't say **What time did you go home**. Also, if we are not at home when we speak, we can't say **I'm coming home**.

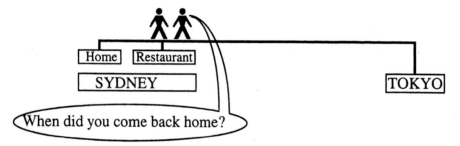

In this case, it is okay to say **When did you come back home**, because home means *Sydney*, not *Tokyo*.

I want to go to sleep.[6]

Go is often used with many words in common day expressions. How many do you know?

Go ~	Meaning
Go to sleep	Begin sleeping.
Go to bed	Enter a bed - maybe for sleeping, maybe not.
Go to work	Go to usual working place.
Go to school	Go to school!
Go out	Opposite of **Come in**. (Also, *go on a date*.)
Go for it	Try hard. Do your best.
Go for a walk/swim	Take/have a swim/walk.
Go (out) for a meal	(= *Eat out*) Eat in a restaurant, not at home.

What's going on?[9]

Go on means *happen*. **What's going on** means *What's happening*. This question is similar to **What are you doing**.

We've been going out for six years.[10]
Go out means *go on a date with* or *become a boyfriend or girlfriend.*
We can also say **Go out with**. Look at the following examples:

Jack is **going out with** Jill. Jack is **going with** Jill. Jack and Jill are **going out**. Jack and Jill are **going out with** each other. Jack and Jill are boyfriend and girlfriend. Jack is *dating* Jill. Jack and Jill are *dating*.	short time or long time
Jack is *going on a date* with Jill.	one time

Go ahead.[11]/Here you are / Help yourself
Go ahead means *Sure* or *It's okay to do that.* We often say **go ahead** when giving permission. Look at the following examples.

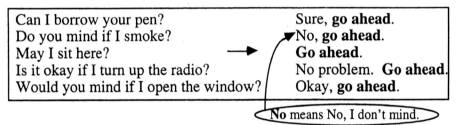

Can I borrow your pen? Do you mind if I smoke? May I sit here? Is it okay if I turn up the radio? Would you mind if I open the window?	Sure, **go ahead**. No, **go ahead**. **Go ahead**. No problem. **Go ahead**. Okay, **go ahead**.

No means No, I don't mind.

There are two other similar expressions. If we give something to somebody, we say **Here you are**. Look at the examples:

Can I borrow your pen? Please pass me my keys. Have you got a light?	Sure. **Here you are**. Okay. **Here you are**. Yeah. **Here you are**.

The other expression is similar. If somebody asks for something, we don't give it to them, but let them take it themselves. In that case, we say **Help yourself**.
For example:

Can I borrow a pen? May I have some sugar, please? That cake looks nice!	Sure. **Help yourself**. Okay. **Help yourself**. Thanks. **Help yourelf**.

Has he come down with a cold?[12]
Come down with means *catch*. It is used with *colds, headaches, the 'flu* etc.
For example, **I've come down with the 'flu** means *I've caught the 'flu* or *I've got the 'flu.*

♪⊚🎥

14 - 5. Student Exercises: Fill in the blanks.
Choose the best sentence from the list below.

1	**Charles:**	Hello. [_____]
2	**Dianna:**	No. [_____]
3	**Charles:**	Oh, please. [_____]
4	**Dianna:**	Allright.
5	**Charles:**	May I ask you a question?
6	**Dianna:**	Okay. [_____]
7	**Charles:**	[_____]
8	**Dianna:**	[_____]
9	**Charles:**	But Diana, didn't you ever love me?
10	**Dianna:**	Ouch! [_____]
11	**Charles:**	'Sorry about your headache but please answer my question.
12	**Dianna:**	[_____] Goodbye.

Choose the best sentences for the blanks.

a) Go away!

b) Go ahead.

c) I'm sorry too Charles, but I want to go to sleep.

d) Well, why did you start going out with me?

e) Come on, Diana!

f) May I come in?

g) I've come down with a terrible headache.

h) What a stupid question! Go back home, Charles!

14 - 6. Student Exercise: Select the best answer.

1. **Enter** is the same as:
   (a) Come on.   (b) Come in.
   (c) Come down.   (d) Come home.

2. **I come from Nohobby** is the same as:
   (a) I'm from Nohobby.   (b) I'm coming from Nohobby.
   (c) I come by Nohobby.   (d) I came to Nohobby.

3. **Go away** means:
   (a) Don't come near me.   (b) Leave (for a long time).
   (c) Leave (forever)   (d) All answers are okay.

4. **Come on** means:
   (a) Hurry up.   (b) You can do it!
   (c) I'm asking you - please!   (d) All answers are okay.

5. If you are at home when you are talking, you *cannot* say:
   (a) I went home at 6.   (b) I came home at 6.
   (c) I got home at 6.   (d) I arrived home at 6.

6. **What's going on** means:
   (a) Where are you going?   (b) What are you going on?
   (c) What's happening?   (d) All answers are bad.

7. **Peter is going out with Wendy** is the same as:
   (a) Peter is dating Wendy.   (b) Peter is going away with Wendy.
   (c) Peter is going ahead   (d) Peter and Wendy are going
   with Wendy.   outside.

8. Instead of saying **It's okay to do that,** we can say:
   (a) Go ahead.   (b) Go away.
   (c) Come on.   (d) All answers are bad.

9. Instead of saying **I've caught a bad cold,** we can say:
   (a) I've come to a bad cold.   (b) I've come into a bad cold.
   (c) I've come out of a bad   (d) I've come down with a bad
   cold.   cold.

10. When somebody says **Please lend me your car,** you give them the keys
    and say:
    (a) Here you are.   (b) Here it is.
    (c) Here we go.   (d) Here it comes.

14 - 7. Review of this lesson's major points. Do you understand these sentences
words and expressions?

Couch	Go back home	Go for a swim	Go out with
Couch potato	Go to sleep	Go for a walk	Go with
Come in.	Go to bed	What's going on?	Go out
Come into	Go to work	Go ahead.	Date
Come down with	Go to school	Here you are.	Go on a date
Come on!	Go for it!	Help yourself.	Go away!
Come here!	Go (out) for a meal		

14 - 8. Student Exercise: Can you see the hidden answer on the next page?

David:	I love lying on the sofa and watching TV.
Charlie:	Do you eat or drink anything while you are watching?
David:	Sure. I usually drink a few beers and eat pizza.
Charlie:	Pizza? By the way, do you know the size of the largest pizza in the world?
David:	No. How big was it?
Charlie:	Well . . . it was made in South Africa in 1990 and it's diameter was (. . . . .) metres!

To find out the size of the pizza, please look at the stereogram carefully:

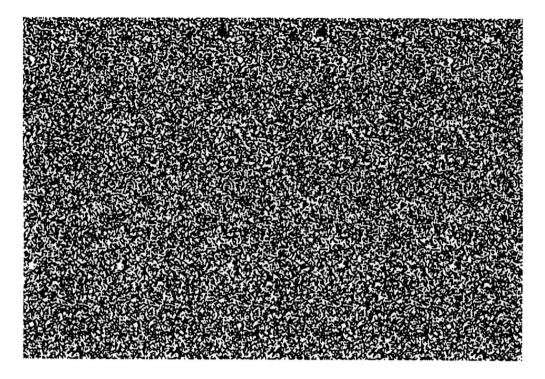

How big was the world's largest pizza? _____

14 - 9. Student Exercise: On the next page is a list of couch potato words. Can you find all of them in the word search below? Words are hidden horizontally - (left to right), vertically - (top to bottom) and diagonally - (top left to bottom right). Target time is **two minutes**.

```
W  S  L  E  E  P  S  O  F  A  R  Q
A  S  M  O  K  E  S  V  I  D  E  O
T  S  V  F  P  U  K  C  V  M  L  G
C  Z  M  A  J  T  B  E  E  R  A  P
H  G  X  C  U  S  H  I  O  N  X  I
C  O  U  C  H  P  O  T  A  T  O  Z
T  E  L  E  V  I  S  I  O  N  S  Z
S  N  O  O  Z  E  L  U  G  O  I  A
A  S  H  T  R  A  Y  E  A  T  T  L
G  J  S  A  D  R  I  N  K  H  C  T
J  U  N  K  F  O  O  D  L  A  Z  Y
R  H  O  B  B  Y  M  A  N  L  I  E
```

Ashtray	Eat	Pizza	Snooze
Beer	Hobbyman	Relax	Sofa
Couchpotato	Junkfood	Sit	Television
Cushion	Lazy	Sleep	Video
Drink	Lie	Smoke	Watch

14 - 10. Student exercise: How well did you understand the first dialogue? Answer the following questions with **true** (T) or **false** (F). Circle the correct answer.

1. We don't know the couch potato's name. (T) or (F)

2. The couch potato is very friendly. (T) or (F)

3. The couch potato wants to go to sleep. (T) or (F)

4. He has a girlfriend. (T) or (F)

5. They've been going out together for 7 years. (T) or (F)

6. The couch potato has come down with a bad cold. (T) or (F)

7. The couch potato never goes anywhere. (T) or (F)

8. The couch potato is 29 years old. (T) or (F)

9. The couch potato is very lazy. (T) or (F)

10. The world's heaviest potato was 3.1 kilograms. (T) or (F)

NOTES:

....

....

....

....

....

15: REVIEW

REVIEW OF LANGUAGE NOTES: Chapter 1 - 14.

CHAPTER ONE:

Lesson Focus: The question word **how**
Hobby theme: Guitar

How' you doing?[1]   (Page 7)
How' you doing is the same as **How are you**. Also, **How's it going** and
How's everything.

Good thanks.[2]   (Page 7)
Answer to **How' you doing**. Other answers include **okay**, **not bad**, **pretty
good**, **good**, **fairly good**, **well**, **great**, **fine**, etc. We can also answer *I'm*
good,**Good** *thanks,* or *I'm* **good** *thanks.*

How about you?[3]   (Page 7)
How about you means *And you?* **How about whisky** means *And whisky?* We
can also say **What about you**.

How come you're wearing that cape?[4]   (Page 8)
How come means *Why.* **How come you're wearing that cape** means *Why are
you wearing that cape*. **How come you're not . . .** means *Why aren't you . . .*

How do you do?[5]   (Page 8)
When we meet somebody for the first time, we often shake hands and say **How
do you do**. We can also say (**It's**) **nice/good/great to meet you** or (**I'm**)
pleased/ happy/glad to meet you.

How did you come here?[6]   (Page 8)
This is the basic **How** sentence. We can use it with any **verb**. This **How** means
By what method or *In what way.*

How many strings are there?[7]   (Page 8)
How many and **How much** both refer to *number*. **How many** refers to things
that we *can count*. **How much** refers to things that we *can't count*.

How old were you when you started playing?[8] (Page 9)
Other phrases, such as **How old** or **How long** refer to *age* or *time* or *length*.

How do you like the guitar?[9] (Page 9)
We can ask peoples' opinions by saying **How do you like . . . ?**

How about a coffee?[10] (Page 9)
We can also use **How about** as an invitation. For example, **How about a coffee** means *Would you like a coffee.*

See ya' around.[11] (Page 9)
See ya' around means *Good-Bye* .We can also say **See ya' 'round** (See you around), **See ya' 'bout** (See you about), **See ya' later** (See you later), **Catch ya' later** (Catch you later) or **Check ya' later** (Check you later).

CHAPTER TWO:

Lesson Focus: The question word **what**
Hobby theme: Surfing

What's happening?[1] (Page 17)
What's happening is a fairly common (American) greeting. It is similar to **How' you doing** or **How' you going** etc. The answer is **Not much, Nothing much** or **Nothing special.**

What about you?[2] (Page 17)
What about you is the same as **How about you.**

What are you doing?[3] (Page 17)
This is the basic **What** question. We can use it with any verb. Explanation should not be necessary.

What?[4] (Page 18)
If somebody speaks to you and you can't hear them, you can say **What**? This is not very polite, but it is common. More polite is **I beg your pardon** or **Pardon me** etc.

What for?[5] (Page 18)
What for means *Why*. Use **What for** only where the previous sentence was *positive*, or did not contain the word *not*.

Say what?[6] (Page 19)
Say what is the same as **What**? **Say what** is very casual American slang. Some people never use this expression - some people use it very often.

What brings you to Earth?[7]   (Page 19)
What brings you to . . . is the same as *Why did you come to . . .?*.
What took you to . . . is the same as *Why did you go to . . . ?*.

What do you think of surfing?[8]   (Page 19)
We can ask peoples opinions by saying **What do you think of . . .?** We can
also say **What do you think about . . . ?** This is similar do *How do you like . .*

What do you mean by "surfing"?[9]   (Page 19)
If you don't understand a word, you can say **What do you mean by. . .** or
What does . . . mean?

What's wrong?[10]   (Page 19)
If somebody has a problem, we often say **What's wrong?** This is the same as
What's the problem, What's the matter, What's up, What's the trouble and
What happened.

CHAPTER THREE:

Lesson Focus: The verb **take**
Hobby theme: Cards

This lesson focuses on the word **take**. **Take** has many meanings. In language
notes 1 to 8, **have** can be used instead of **take**. The meaning is the same.

Take a seat.[1]   (Page 27)
Take a seat means *have a seat* or *sit down.*

We're taking a break now.[2]   (Page 27)
Take a break means *have a break, rest* or *relax for a short time.*

Simon's taking a shower.[3]   (Page 27)
Take a shower means *have a shower* or *wash in a shower.*

John's taking a walk.[4]   (Page 27)
Take a walk means *have a walk* or *go for a walk.*

Glenn's taking a pee.[5]   (Page 27)
Take a pee means *have a pee* or *go to the toilet.*

Do you take off anytime for dinner?[6]   (Page 27)
Take of time means *have off time* or *rest* or *relax.*

We usually take 5 or 10 minutes.[7]   (Page 27)
Take 5 means *rest* or *relax for a short time*. The same as **have 5 minutes (off)**.

Take a look at this![8]   (Page 27)
Take a look means *have a look* or *look at*.

Do you take milk (or **sugar**) **in your tea?**   (Page 27)
Take milk means *have milk* or *put milk (or sugar) in your drink*.

Let's take a bath!   (Page 27)
Take a bath means *have a bath* or *get into a bath* or *wash in a bath*.

Take it easy, Hobbyman![9]   (Page 28)
Take it easy means **Relax** or **Don't worry**.

I first took part in a game 10 years ago.[10]   (Page 28)
Take part in means *participate*, *join in* or *play* (in the case of games & sports).

My father took me to Las Vegas.[11]   (Page 28)
Take means *carry*, or *go with a person, an animal or an object from one place* (near the speaker) *to another place* (far from the speaker). **Take** is the opposite of bring.

It took over 10 hours![12]   (Page 29)
Take is often used with *time*. e.g. From Tokyo to Sydney by plane **takes** 9 hrs.

We took home $2000.[13]   (Page 29)
Take home or **bring home** means *carry home*.

I take after him.[14]   (Page 29)
Take after means *look like* or *be like*. e.g. She **takes after** her mother.

My mother couldn't take his gambling.[15]   (Page 29)
Can't take means *can't stand* or *can't endure*. **Can take** means *can endure*.

I'm sorry I took up your time.[16]   (Page 29)
Take up is often used with *time*. The expression **I'm sorry I took up your time** is often used to finish a (business) conversation.

Take care![17]   (Page 29)
Take care (**of yourself**) means *Be careful and don't do anything dangerous*. It's a very common greeting, when leaving friends.

Take[18]   (Page 29)
Take can also mean *Steal*. e.g. **He took my bike** means *He stole my bike*.

CHAPTER FOUR:

Lesson Focus: The verb **have**
Hobby theme: Beermaking

(Page 37)

I have a bad hangover.[1] **Why do you have a red face?**[3] **If I have a cold . . .**[8]
When we talk about our *body*, *sickness* or *health*, we often use the word **have**.
In conversation, we often say **have got** instead of **have**.

I have a nice hobby.[2]/ **How many different beers do you have?**[7]   (Page 37)
This **have** refers to *ownership*. It is very common. We *can* also use **have got**
instead of **have** in this case.

Last night I had a meeting.[4]   (Page 37)
We use the word "have" when many people gather together. e.g. **have a party,**
have a meeting, have a tennis lesson or **have a wedding reception** etc.

We had many different beers.[5]   (Page 38)
Have is often used with eating and drinking. e.g. **have something to drink,**
have something to eat, have two pies, have a drink or **have 2 beers.** We
can't use **have got** instead of **have** in this case.

I had a really good time, thanks.[6]   (Page 38)
Have a good time is the same as *enjoy oneself.* e.g. **She had a good time**
means *She enjoyed herself.* We *can't* use **have got** instead of **have** in this case.

If I have a fight with my wife . .[8] **My wife had a baby last month.**[11] (Page 38)
Have is a very useful verb. If you are not sure what verb to use, try using **have.**
e.g. **have a fight, have a dream, have an accident** or **Have a nice day!**
In most of these cases, we *can't* use **have got** instead of **have**.

You have a wife?[9] **I also have a dog.**[10]   (Page 38-9)
We use the word **have** for *family members, friends* and *pets* etc. We *can* use
have got instead of **have** in this case. (*But only present tense.*)

Do you have a light?[12]/ **I have no idea.**[13]   (Page 39)
Some **have** sentences are very common in *slang* daily conversation. e.g. **'Got a**
light?, 'You got the time? and **'Got a smoke?** etc.

CHAPTER FIVE:

Lesson Focus: **There is/are, Too many/much, Not enough, Likes/dislikes**
Hobby theme: Swimming

What do you like doing in your spare time?[1]   (Page 47)
Instead of saying *My hobby is . . .* , we often say **I like . . . ing in my spare time**. We can also say **I like . . . ing in my free time** or **I'm interested in . . .**

I'm crazy about it![2] **It's okay.**[6] **I can't stand it.**[8]   (Page 47)

I like it.	*I don't like it.*	*It's so-so.*
I'm crazy about it.	I can't stand it.	It's allright.
I love it.	I hate it.	It's okay.
I think it's great.	It really sucks.	It's reasonable.

There aren't any swimmers.[3]   (Page 48)
There aren't . . . or **there isn't** means that something does not exist. e.g.
There aren't any flies in China.
When the sentence is about a *person, people* or *a country* etc, we can often use *have* instead of **there isn't/aren't**. e.g. *I don't have a bath in my house* is the same as **There isn't a bath in my house.**

There are 4 major strokes.[4]   (Page 48)
There are . . . or **there is . . .** means that something exists. *Single* and *uncountable* objects use **there is** and *plural* objects use **there are**.
Sometimes we can use *have* instead of **there is/are**.   (See example above).

Aren't there any more?[5]   (Page 49)
To make questions, **There is** becomes **Is there**, **There are** becomes **Are there**, **There isn't** becomes **Isn't there** and **There aren't** becomes **Aren't there**.
Have can be used instead of **isn't/aren't there** in some cases.

It's too slow.[7] **It's too difficult!**[9]   (Page 49)
When we use the word **too** with adjectives or adverbs, **too** comes *before* the adjective or adverb. e.g. **He's too small. You write too slowly!**

There are always too many people.[10] **It costs too much money.**[11]   (Page 49)
When we use the word **too** with nouns, we also have to use **many** with *countable* nouns, and **much** with *uncountable* nouns. These words come *before* the noun.
e.g. **You have too much money. He has too many girlfriends.**
We can also use **too** with verbs. In this case, we also have to use the word **much**. **Too much** comes *after* the verb. e.g. **You cry too much!**

There aren't enough pretty girls.[12]   (Page 50)
The opposite of **too** or **too much** is **not enough**. **Not enough** means that the *number* or *amount* is too small. e.g. **It's not hot enough, today. We never eat enough.**

CHAPTER SIX:

Lesson Focus:　　The words **it, that & one**
Hobby theme:　　Snowboarding

It's a nice day![1]　　　　　　　　　　　　　　　　　　(Page 57)
We often use the word **it** when we are talking about the weather. e.g. **It's a nice day, today.**

That's right.[2] **That's cheap!**[9] **That's good!**[11] **That's okay.**[13]　(Page 57)
That is a very, very useful word and there are many common "**that sentences**".
e.g.　**That's right! That's cheap! That's good! That's okay/ That's allright. That's too bad! That's terrible!** etc.

It's good to meet you, too.[3]　　　　　　　　　　　　(Page 58)
Don't confuse the "**It's** greetings" and the "**I'm** greetings". (See Lesson 1, p.8)

I started it about 6 years ago.[4]　**I first bought one 5 years ago.**[5]　(Page 58)
Do you like snowboarding?　　Yes, I like **it**.
Do you have a snowboard?　　Yes, I have **one**.
Are they new boots?　　　　　Yes, I just bought **them**.

Before that,[6]　　　　　　　　　　　　　　　　　　(Page 58)
That is also used with *time*. We often say **before that, . . .** or **after that, . . .**

It was about $300.[7] **They were only $90.**[8]　　　　　(Page 59)
It is often used with *money*. *Plural* nouns use **they**. e.g. **It's $300. They are only $90.** *Time* also uses **It**. e.g. **It's 3 o'clock.**

This one is 1.6 metres.[10]　　　　　　　　　　　　　(Page 59)
One (meaning *a single item or person*) is often used with **this** and **that**. e.g. **This one's mine, and that one's his.** We use **ones** for *plural* objects. e.g. **Red cars are nice, but I like black ones.**

That's my friend Simms.[12]　　　　　　　　　　　　(Page 59)
When introducing people, we often say **Mr A, this is Mr B**. If the person is *not* standing close to us, we often use **That**. e.g. **That's my wife.**

CHAPTER SEVEN:

Lesson Focus:　　The verb **get**
Hobby theme:　　Martial Arts

How did you get into martial arts?[1] (Page 67)
Get into means *become involved in* or *become interested in.* e.g. **When did you get into making movies, Steven?**

When I got to school, . . .[2] **I get home at 9.**[11] (Page 67)
Get sometimes means *arrive at* or *reach.* e.g. **I get to school at 8.30.**

"We're gonna' get you!"[3] (Page 67)
(slang) **We're gonna' get you** means *We are going to get you.* In this case, **. . . going to get . . .** means **tease, hurt** or **punish**.

Oh - I get it![4] (Page 67)
I get it means *I understand.* Also, *I follow you* and *I'm with you.* **I don't get it** means *I don't understand.* (The same as *I don't follow you* or *I'm not with you.*)

I always got away.[5] (Page 68)
Get away has 2 meanings in English conversation. One meaning is *escape*. The other meaning, used as a command, is *Don't come here* or *Don't go there.*

I got a really bad cold.[6] (Page 68)
We can use **get** when we talk about *health*. In this case, **get** means *catch* or *have*.

I couldn't get over it.[7] (Page 68)
Get over means *get well* or *recover from.* We use **get over** when we talk about *physical* or *emotional* problems. e.g. **I just can't get over this bad cold.**

When I got out of hospital, . . .[8] **I gotta' get out a' here.**[13] (Page 68)
Get out (of) means *leave.* e.g. **When does Mike get out of prison?**

Get fit and healthy.[9] (Page 68)
Get also means *become.* e.g. **John got old and weak.** ➔*John became old and weak.*

I get up at 6.[10] (Page 69)
Get up means *get out of bed.*

It's getting late . . .[12] (Page 69)
It's getting late means *It's becoming late.* This expression is used when somebody wants to leave a group of people or go back home.

Where did you get that cape?[14] **I got it from my mother.**[15] (Page 69)
Get can mean *acquire, buy* or *find.* e.g. **Where did you get that beautiful silk dress?**

CHAPTER EIGHT:

Lesson Focus: The verb **give**
Hobby theme: Tennis

Give me a hand with this heavy bag.[1]   (Page 77)
Give a hand has 2 meanings in conversational English. One meaning is *help*. The other meaning is *clap* or *applaud*. e.g. **This is heavy. Give me a hand!**

Given name[2]   (Page 77)

first name **given name** Christian name	last name surname family name

Give me a hint![3]   (Page 77)
Hint uses the word **give**. If we want a **hint**, we say **Give me a hint please.**

Boris gives the ball to Hobbyman.[4]   (Page 78)
There are two ways of making the same sentence using **give**. It is okay to use **it** in the first type of sentence, (i.e. *person-give-thing-to-person*), but NOT in the second type of sentence, (i.e. *person-give-person-thing*). It IS okay to use **that** in both types of sentences. e.g. **I gave that to him** & **I gave him that**.

Give me a break![5]   (Page 78)
Give me a break means *Don't tease me* or *Let me relax* or *Don't ask me any questions*. **Give me . . .** is sometimes shortened to *Gimme'* . . . , so people sometimes say **Gimme' a break**.

Give me more time.[6]   (Page 78)
When we *need more time*, or *set time limits*, we often use the word **give**. e.g. *Give* me 2 more days - **I can't finish today**. I can't *give* you any more time.

Are you kidding?[7]   (Page 79)
Kidding means *joking*, so **Are you kidding** means *Are you joking*. This is a very common expression in everyday conversation. Another similar, good expression is *Are you serious*.

Why are you giving me such a hard time?[8]   (Page 79)
Give a hard time means *tease* or *torment*. This expression is very common.

I give up![9]   (Page 79)
Give up is a very useful verb, and has many meanings. One meaning is *admit defeat* (*physical* or *mental*). So, I **give up** means *Okay - you win* or *I have no idea*. In this case, **give in** is the same.
The second meaning is *stop* or *quit*. (**Give in** *can't* be used in this case.)

The third meaning is *lose hope*. (**Give in** also *can't* be used in this case.)

And please give me back my ball![10]   (Page 79)
Give back means *return something to it's owner*. e.g. **I gave it back to him**.

Give me a call.[11]   (Page 79)
Give me a call means *please call me by phone*. Other phone verbs are *call, phone, ring, give a ring* etc.

You didn't give me your phone number.[12]   (Page 80)
Give me sometimes means *tell me*. e.g. **Please give me his name again**.
Sometimes we can use **Let me know** - the meaning is similar.

CHAPTER NINE:

Lesson Focus: The verbs **talk, say, speak & tell**
Hobby theme: Computing

Are you talking to me?[1] **Who's speaking?**[2]   (Page87)
Talking and **speaking** are similar. Both words use either **to** or **with** to show
the object. e.g. **I talked *with* him. He spoke *to* us**.

Who said that?[3]   (Page 88)
Say or **said** is used with people's spoken words. e.g. **What did he say?**
Say is also used with *direct* and *indirect* sentences. Look at this summary:

Sentences:		**A said**	**(that)**	**S**	**V(past)**	**O**
	(I)	John said	(that)	he	was buying	a new car
	(D)	John said		"I	am buying	a new car."
Questions(1):		**A asked B**	**W?**	**S**	**V(past)**	**O**
	(I)	John asked me	when	I	was going	to Tokyo.
	(D)	John said	"When	are you	going	to Tokyo?"
Questions(2):		**A asked B**	**IF**	**S**	**V(past)**	**O**
	(I)	John asked me	if	I	liked	cabbage.
	(D)	John said	"Do	you	like	cabbage?"
Commands(1):		**A told B**	**TO**		**V(present)**	**O**
	(I)	John told me	to		go	home.
	(D)	John said			"Go	home"
Commands(2):		**A told B**	**NOT TO**		**V(present)**	**O**
	(I)	John told me	not to		watch	TV.
	(D)	John said	"Don't		watch	TV!"

Please tell me your name![4]   (Page 89)
Tell is often used for *information*. e.g. **Tell me where you met her** or
He told me his address.

You can't tell (that) it's a computer.[5]   (Page 89)
Can't tell (that) means *we can't know the truth about something by looking or
listening*. e.g. **Is that a soccerball or a volleyball? I can't tell.**

Please tell me about it.[6]   (Page 89)
Tell someone about is similar to **tell** (*Language Note 4*), but the topic of
conversation is wider. e.g. **Tell me about your family.**

When I was a kid, my father always talked about computers.[7]   (Page 89)
Talk about means *discuss*. **Let's talk about soccer** means *Let's discuss
soccer.*

They say (that) most jobs use computers.[8]   (Page 89)
They say (that) . . . is the same as *It is said* . . . . This means that *something is
widely believed*, or that *most people think it is true*. e.g. **They say it'll rain
tomorrow.**

Would you say (that) computer's will take peoples' jobs?[9]   (Page 89)
Would you say . . . means *Do you think* . . . . The answer is **I'd say . . .**, which
means *I think . . .*

Shall we talk it over with Mac?[10]   (Page 90)
Talk . . . over means *discuss problems* or *serious things.*

Let's ask Mac.[11]   (Page 90)
Ask is the question verb.

Generally speaking, computers are user-friendly.[12]   (Page 90)
Generally speaking . . . means *in most cases* or *usually*. e.g. **Generally
speaking, Japanese people have black hair.**

Speaking of time . . .[13]   (Page 90)
Speaking of . . . is used when we want to *change the conversation topic.*

CHAPTER TEN:

Lesson Focus: The verbs **see, watch & look**
Hobby theme: Rollerblades

That looks dangerous![1]   (Page 97)
Looks is often used with adjectives. **That looks dangerous** means *That seems*

(or appears) dangerous. **Look like** (not **look**) is used with nouns.

I can't see them very well.[2]   (Page 97)
See is the basic *'eye-verb'*. It means *notice with the eye.* **See** is often used with
can. Other words, such as *look* or *watch* rarely use **can.**

Take a closer look.[3] **You should look where you're going!**[10]   (Page 97)
Look means *pay attention to a particular object.* **Take a look** or **have a look**
has the same meaning, but the *time is shorter.* e.g. **Look at that big horse!**

They look like ice-skates.[4]   (Page 97)
Look like is used with nouns. **He looks like a pro-wrestler** means *He seems or
appears to be a pro-wrestler.* We *can't* use **look** by itself with nouns.

Let me see . . .[5]   (Page 98)
Let me see . . . is used while we are thinking, or not sure what to say. It is the
same as *Ah . . . , Um . . . , Well . . .* and *Er . . . .*

I see.[6]   (Page 98)
I see means *I understand.* If somebody explains something to you, you can say
I see what you mean.

Watch this![7]   (Page 98)
Watch means *look carefully for a length of time, usually for a purpose.* We
often use the word **watch** with *TV, shows, games, presentations* etc.

Look out![8] **I told you to watch out.**[9]   (Page 98)
Look out and **watch out** are warnings. They mean *Be careful* or *Danger.*

Let's look for them.[11]   (Page 98)
Look for is the same as *search for* or *hunt.* e.g. **I've lost my keys. Please
help me look for them.**

I think you should see a doctor.[12]   (Page 98)
See sometimes means *visit* or *meet.* We often use **see** when we *make
an appointment* with someone. We also use **see** when we *visit* or *meet* friends.

My mother will look after me.[13]   (Page 99)
Look after means *care for* or *take care of.* e.g. **Who's looking after the baby?**

I'll see you later.[14]   (Page 99)
Instead of saying *Good bye,* we can say **See you** or **See you later.** *(For other
alternatives, see Language Notes 1 - 4 - 11, page 9).*

CHAPTER ELEVEN:

Lesson Focus: **Almost / Nearly / Just about**
Hobby theme: Fishing

I go fishing on almost every Sunday.[1] (Page 107)
Almost, nearly and **just about** are the same. We often use these words with
all, every, no, none or **any**. **Almost all boys** means *about 90% of boys*.
Almost no boys means *about 10% of boys*.

Nearly all fishermen get up early.[2] (Page 108)
Nearly all fishermen get up early means *Most fishermen get up early*. **Almost**
is not the same as *most*. **Almost all** is the same as *most*.

Almost nobody catches any fish if they come late.[3] (Page 108)
Almost nobody catches any fish if they come late means *Most people who
come late cannot catch any fish*. (*See Language Note 1*).

Well, almost always.[4] (Page 108)
Almost always means *usually*. **Almost never** means *hardly ever* or *rarely*.

I'm almost finished for today.[5] (Page 108)
Almost, just about or **nearly** can also mean that *an action has almost finished*,
or *a change has been completed*. e.g. **I'm almost finished** means *I will be
finished soon*. **He's almost dead** means *He will be dead soon* or *He is close to
death*.

(Page 108)
Almost one year ago, I was fishing here.[6] **It was just about sunrise.**[7]
Almost one year ago means *about one year ago* or *just under one year ago*. **It
was nearly sunrise** means *It was about sunrise*.

It almost got away.[8] (Page 109)
Almost, just about and **nearly** can also mean that *an action looked like being
completed, but was not completed*. **The fish almost got away** means *we
thought the fish would escape, but it didn't*. **Note: Always** use *past tense* in
this type of sentence.

It nearly pulled me in the river.[9] (Page 109)
It nearly pulled me in the river means *I thought it might pull me in the river,
but it didn't*. (*See Language Note 8*)

I almost caught another large fish.[10] (Page 109)
I almost caught another large fish means *I thought I would catch another big
fish, but I couldn't*. (*See Language Note 8*)

Most of the fish that I caught today are pretty small.[11]   (Page 109)
Most sometimes needs to use **of**. If we use **the, these, that, my, your, his** etc, we have to use **of**. e.g. **I've seen** *most of this movie*. *Most of his hair* **is grey.**

Most guys say that good bait is the most important.[13]   (Page 109)
If we don't use **the, these, that, my, your, his** etc, we don't need **of**. e.g. **Most foreigners like sushi.**   Never say **Most** *of* **foreigners like sushi.**

What is the most important thing in fishing?[12]   (Page 110)
The most can also be used with adjectives over 2 syllables.   e.g. **I think America is** *the most dangerous* **country.**

CHAPTER TWELVE:

Lesson Focus: **Numbers**
Hobby theme: Cars

It's a '93 model (*ninety three*) **Cherokee.**[1]   (Page 117)
We often shorten years to the last two numbers, in daily conversation. e.g. **I was born in '55** (fifty five).

It was about 4 000 000 (*four million*) **yen.**[3]   (Page 117)
The English number system is easy to understand. **1 000 000 = One million. 1 000 000 000 = One billion. 1 000 000 000 000 = One trillion.**

4 *mil!*[4] **In America, it costs about 25** *thou.*[2]   (Page 118)
In conversation, **million** is often shortened to *mil.* In the same way, **thousand** is often shortened to *thou.*

It was about 3.8 million (*three point eight million*) **plus tax.**[5]   (Page 118)
With large numbers, (more than one million), we often use **a decimal point.**
e.g.   **5 710 000   = 5.71 million (five point seven one million)**

It does about 6.3 km/l (*six point three kilometres per litre*)**.**[6]   (Page 118)
The mark "/" is read **per.** e.g. **km/l**   =   kilometres **per** litre.

19 $\frac{1}{2}$ (*nineteen and a half*) **miles per gallon.**[7]   (Page 119)
Fractions are easy to read: e.g   two thirds $\longrightarrow$ $\frac{2}{3}$

eight and three quarters $\longrightarrow$ $8\frac{3}{4}$

Top speed is about 190 .[8] **I had a Benz 190 .**[9]   (Page 119)
Numbers with three or four digits are often read a special way. For example:
160 km/h. (**one sixty**) 185 cm (**one eighty five**) Room 1520 (**fifteen twenty**)

I have a 1908 (*nineteen oh eight*) **T Model Ford.**[10]   (Page 119)
We can't shorten years that have the number *zero* in them.
(*See Language Note 1.*) The *zero* becomes **oh** e.g. **1906 - nineteen oh six**

My number is 551-2333 (*double five one, two triple three*).[11]   (Page 119)
When saying phone numbers, we often say **double** or **triple**. Also, similar to
years (*Language Note 10*), *zero* is usually pronounced **oh**.

I have a driving lesson at 6:05 (*six oh five*).[12]   (Page 120)
When we tell the time, *zero* is also pronounced **oh**. e.g. **8:07 = eight oh seven.**

CHAPTER THIRTEEN:

Lesson Focus: **Negative questions**
Hobby theme: Mountain Bikes

You're not from Earth, are you?[1] **No, I'm not.**   (Page 127)
This is a *negative tag question* and a *negative* (or **No**) *answer*. The answer
agrees with the question. e.g. **You don't like beer, do you?   No, I don't.**
                                                            (Page 127)
And people on your planet have many hobbies, don't they?[2] **No, they don't.**
This is a *positive tag question* and a *negative* (or **No**) *answer*. The answer
disagrees with the question. e.g. **You like beer, don't you?   No, I don't.**

This isn't a mountain bike, is it?[3] **Yes, it is.**   (Page 128)
This is a *negative tag question* and a *positive* (or **Yes**) *answer*. The answer
disagrees with the question. e.g. **You don't like beer, do you? Yes, I do.**

Mountain bikes are quite new, aren't they Dale?[4] **Yes, they are.** (Page 128)
This is a *positive tag question* and a *positive* (or **Yes**) *answer*. The answer
agrees with the question. e.g. **You like beer, don't you? Yes, I do.**

You don't have any bikes on the planet Nohobby?[5]   (Page 128)
In conversation, we can make a question by using a *negative* or *positive*
sentence, with a rising intonation. e.g. **You don't like peanuts?**

People usually just walk, right?[6]   (Page 129)
Right can be used like a **tag**. If you say **right** on the end of a question, you
want people to agree with you. e.g. **You're Ray Charles, right?** **Yes, I am.**

That's right.[7] **That's correct.**[8]   (Page 129)
When we agree with people, we can say **That's right** or **That's correct**.
That's right or **That's correct** can both be used for **agreeing** with a *positive* or
negative question or sentence. They can mean either **Yes** or **No**.
e.g. *You like beer, don't you?* **That's right.** *I love it*!

CHAPTERFOURTEEN:

Lesson Focus:　　The verbs **come & go**
Hobby theme:　　Couch Potato.

May I come in?[1] **A pretty girl comes into the room.**[7]　　(Page 137)
Come in means *enter a room.*. **Come into** also means *enter*.

I come from Nohobby and . . .[2]　　(Page 137)
When we talk about our home town, or where we were born, we often say **I'm from . . .**. We can also say **I come from** . . . .

Go away![3]　　(Page 137)
Go away has 2 meanings. One meaning is *leave* (for a long time, or forever). The second meaning is used as a *command*. It means **Don't come near me**.

Come on![4]　　(Page 137)
Come on has 3 meanings. The first meaning is similar to *Hurry up*. The second meaning is *a form of encouragement*. The third meaning is *Please - I'm asking you* or *I'm requesting you*. **Come on** does *not* mean **come here**.

Go back home![5] **Come here!**[8] **He never goes anywhere.**[13]　　(Page 137)
Go and **come** are basic words in English conversation, but are often confused. If we are at home when we speak, we can't say **What time did you go home**. Also, if we are not at home when we speak, we can't say **I'm coming home**.

I want to go to sleep.[6]　　(Page 138)
Go is often used with many words in common everyday day expressions. e.g. **Go to sleep, Go to bed, Go to work, Go to school, Go for it, Go for a walk/swim** etc.

What's going on?[9]　　(Page 138)
Go on means *happen*. **What's going on** means *What's happening*. This question is similar to **What are you doing**.

We've been going out for six years.[10]　　(Page 139)
Go out means *go on a date with* or *become a boyfriend or girlfriend*. We can also say **Go out with**.

Go ahead.[11]　　(Page 139)
Go ahead means *Sure* or *It's okay to do that*. We often say **go ahead** when giving permission. Similar expressions are **Here you are** and **Help yourself**.

Has he come down with a cold?[12]　　(Page 139)
Come down with means *catch*. It is used with colds, headaches, the 'flu etc. e.g. **I've come down with the 'flu** means *I've caught the 'flu* or *I've got the 'flu*.

―――――――――――――――― 著者略歴 ――――――――――――――――

Simon Thollar ソーラ・サイモン
1960年7月生まれ
北海道情報大学　経営情報学部 システム情報学科
教授
1982 年タスマニア公立大学　文学士
1983 年タスマニア公立大学　教育学修士
1987 年タスマニア公立大学　特別支援教育修士
2004 年シェフィールド大学（英国）日本文化論修士

主たる研究業績

「SpeakOut!」第2版発行 丸善プラネット株式会社 2003

「Hobbyman 」第2版発行 丸善プラネット株式会社 2003

「Simon Says」初版発行 丸善プラネット株式会社 2019

「Does being "globally minded" facilitate English learning in universty students?」
韓国英語教育学会（KOTESOL）年次国際大会Proceeding 2018

「Transitions in Faculty Awareness: Exploring What University Students Don't Like About Teachers＿
韓国英語教育学会（KOTESOL）年次国際大会Proceedings 2016

「Applying digital game-based language learning to improve /l/ and /r/ phoneme discrimination」
韓国英語教育学会（KOTESOL）年次国際大会Proceedings 2015

「Motivating Students With Humorous One-Point Videos.」
JALT2012 Conference Proceedings. Oct 12-15, 2012, Tokyo: JALT, pp.506-515. 2013

「The Application of Entertaining, One-Point Videos in Remedial English Education」
北海道情報大学紀要論文 第25巻1号，pp.1-14. 2013

「Improving teaching skills and strategies through awareness of individual teaching traits」
北海道情報大学紀要論文 第24巻2号，pp.15-28.

「The design and construction of a readily accessible on-line student skills taxonomy to quantify abilities」
北海道情報大学紀要論文 第24巻1号，pp.17-32.

「Improving auditory L/R discrimination through the design and implementation of serious games」
北海道情報大学紀要論文 第24巻1号，pp.1-15.

Hobbyman-Easy English Conversation with an Alien　3rd edition

―――――――――――――――――――――――――――――――

2024年1月30日　初版発行

―――――――――――――――――――――――――――――――

著　　者　Simon Thollar　　　©2024

―――――――――――――――――――――――――――――――

発 行 所　**丸善プラネット株式会社**
　　　　　〒101-0051　東京都千代田区神田神保町二丁目17 番
　　　　　電話 (03) 3512-8516
　　　　　https://maruzenplanet.hondana.jp

発 売 所　**丸善出版株式会社**
　　　　　〒101-0051　東京都千代田区神田神保町二丁目17 番
　　　　　電話 (03) 3512-3256
　　　　　https://www.maruzen-publishing.co.jp

―――――――――――――――――――――――――――――――

組版・印刷・製本　株式会社留萌新聞　印刷事業部あるふぁらんど

―――――――――――――――――――――――――――――――

ISBN　978-4-86345-557-3 C0082